INTRODUCTION

Welcome to a new concept in cooking – the concept of Pure & Simple. The approach is about simplicity and purity, not only in the ingredients but also in the frame of mind while preparing food.

It is based on the appreciation that food is very sensitive to energy vibrations and, as we ingest the food, so too we ingest those same vibrations. In other words, food prepared whilst feeling hurried will perpetuate within us the sense of having to rush. Likewise, if we allow ourselves to feel irritated about something during the process of cooking, then we are likely to keep on thinking the same thoughts whilst that food is within our body!

The ideal way to prepare food is therefore to have calm and very few thoughts. A simple, easy to follow recipe makes this easier to achieve. All recipes are vegetarian. The ingredients used are fresh and seasonal wherever possible, "Eat fresh to keep your mind fresh." They are easy to get hold of and any you might be less familiar with have probably been explained on page 246, Ingredients. The preparation methods are plain and quick, with clear instructions, and cooking times are brief. The recipes are skilfully designed to match our changing and versatile lifestyles with dishes that can be adapted for swift suppers, snacks 'to go', packed lunches for school or work. Most dishes can also be combined for a full and satisfying main meal.

Pure & Simple seeks to engage the reader on three levels: physical, mental and holistic, and thus offers triple nourishment.

On a physical level, it provides 108 tried and tested recipes, which are quick and practical to make, in tune with the time most people feel they can spend in their kitchen.

It engages the reader's mind by introducing some creative ideas which may be new to both beginners and expert cooks. It also recognises that recipes, like language, live on down the generations, constantly undergoing change and refinement according to the times.

And on a holistic level, it suggests that preparing and serving food not only sustains the body but holds a deeper significance. How we select and purchase the ingredients, our focus and concentration when we prepare the food, our state of mind when we share it with others - all impact on how it tastes, how much it nourishes and how much we enjoy it.

Based on a healthy lacto-vegetarian diet, Pure & Simple caters for those thinking about becoming vegetarian but unsure where to start, and also for established 'veggies' looking for newness and culinary variety.

The two authors, Isik Polater and Manju Patel, come together to offer a rich culinary heritage.

Hailing from Turkey, the meeting point of East and West and host to many ancient civilisations and cultures, Isik specialises in dishes like artichokes in olive oil and rice with aubergines and almonds and dill. A trained engineer, who has worked actively in business for the last 18 years, Isik brings precision and practicality to the mix. "I like to experiment with and refine my recipes, while simplifying the method," she says. Isik cooks by being focused and concentrated, "I judge how the food looks and smells, rather than tasting it while cooking. This trains my senses and teaches me to be in harmony with what I am doing."

"I feel that cooking offers a wonderful opportunity for creativity and, if you approach it with an open intellect, it offers a secret link to the ones who invented the recipe. Cooking also means touching culture, evaluating it and taking part in it. By cooking and sharing food, you can feel instant happiness for the self and for others." And Isik's secret? "Cook with love, enjoy the activity but be detached from the results. It will turn out just as it's supposed to."

Born in Uganda, but having lived in Britain for most of her life, Manju offers traditional Indian classics, like semolina halva with almonds, with a dash of international flair. Manju is married with three grown-up sons. "Growing up in a close-knit community, where the doors were always warmly open to friends, family and neighbours, I learnt from an early age that sharing food brought about happiness, love and unity. It continues to play an important part in my life today, where I approach cooking as a means to escape the stresses of everyday life."

"With a huge extended family, there's always an opportunity for me to experiment and be creative in what I see as my sanctuary. I'm not a professional cook, clearly illustrated by the fact that I cook for pleasure with my favourite music playing at full volume in the background, but I do have a habit of being organised in the kitchen where I lay out all the ingredients in front of me before I start and make sure I wash up as I go along. Just as my mother encouraged me to help in the cooking from a very young age, I got my sons involved as I recognised there can be so much joy derived in the process, as well as in the end result."

Both Isik and Manju have been meditators using the method of Raja Yoga for many years. And both claim that this practice helps to deal with the challenges of everyday family and working life, and inevitably improves their cooking.

Our thoughts, and the vibrations those thoughts create in the kitchen, are bound to affect the food and, ultimately, those who eat it. We become what we eat, in fact. And, if that is so, it would obviously benefit us to think the best thoughts and put the highest quality of vibrations into our food, as well as the finest and purest ingredients we can find, carefully washed and cleaned, fresh as they can be, and filled with their own pure energy and nourishment.

Any dish prepared in this understanding has the added ingredient 'x' that makes it taste unique. Just think of meals your mother or grandmother gave; no-one else's vegetable soup or apple pie was ever quite the same. Why? They added that magic ingredient – their love.

So, to fully enjoy the flavours within Pure & Simple, prepare yourself before you begin. Planning ahead is essential. Start with spotless work surfaces and lay out shining, clean utensils – honour the 'purity'. Then clear your mind. Today there is a lot of attention on body detox; just sitting still for a moment in reflective stillness beforehand can also help detox the mind of any distracting thoughts.

Next, focus on the task in hand, add each ingredient with care and good wishes for those who will enjoy your food, and follow each step with accuracy. Tidy up as you go along, and especially keep the sink area clear and clean. Use your time wisely, by staying focused on the task. Don't allow distractions such as taking a long phone call. See the kitchen as a spiritual space where art, joy and passion are allowed to reign free and uninterrupted.

Regard cooking as an enjoyable experience, so that you stir into every dish that added 'x' ingredient. And, before you serve the fruits of your labours, send up a thankful thought to the Provider of all.

If you prepare food in such a way, you will have entered the spirit of the Pure & Simple cookbook. Your efforts will be simple and the results simply delicious, a pure delight …

ACKNOWLEDGEMENTS
The authors wish to acknowledge all those who have assisted in the preparation of this book:

Those who contributed their time and their experience; those who scraped and chopped and cooked; those family members who allowed our kitchens to be overrun with trial dishes; those who tested and tasted and made recommendations; those who edited, stirred the sentences and whisked the words; those who photographed, designed and baked the pages; those who sprinkled their support and basted us with encouragement throughout the project. To each and every one – thank you.

And, above all, our thanks to the One to whom we offer all our efforts in cookery and in life, to the Provider of All, the One who sustains and nourishes us all – our loving thanks.

Throughout the ages, and across the geographical regions of the planet, food has been an integral part of celebrating the sacred festivals, honouring the Divine, sharing love with family, friends and neighbours for all occasions.

Planting, sustaining, growing and harvesting food has been the stimulus for Holy Festivals filled with a sense of the sacred and a recognition that the whole process comes not just through human creativity and effort, but also through the support of the elements of Nature and the Grace of the Divine.

Today we can take that to the next step. We may no longer be actively engaged in the planting and harvesting, but in the purchasing, preparing, cooking and serving. Each step can be with mindfulness and a higher awareness.

My family migrated to London from India when I was eight. I, myself, learnt the first basic steps at home in London watching and helping my mother in the kitchen at weekends. Whilst still at school, there were a few simple recipes like rice, lentils and Indian 'chai' – the cooked tea made with fragrant cardamom – that I could proudly prepare.

My first effort at the Indian flat bread, 'roti', looked more like the map of India than the beautiful circles that the experts create. But, the joy of actually creating and producing things that could be offered and shared was a particularly pleasing experience that continues till today.

My hope is that you will experiment with and enjoy these recipes that have been put together by Isik and Manju - not professional cooks, but ones who cook purely and simply for love...

B.K. Jayanti
European Director of the
Brahma Kumaris World Spiritual University

Contents

Unless otherwise stated, all recipes will serve 4-6 people.

This chapter offers a tasty selection of dishes which could be served in small portions as starters and are light enough not to spoil the appetite for the main course, or can be 'up-sized' to main meals.

STARTERS

Aubergine (Eggplant) Slices with Tomatoes

PREPARATION

1   Preheat the oven to 240°C / 500°F / Gas mark 7.

2   Place the aubergine slices in salted water. Leave for 5 minutes. Drain and hand-squeeze until dry (to remove the bitter taste).

3   Place the aubergine slices on an oiled oven tray and sprinkle some of the olive oil on top. Season with freshly ground black pepper and some of the thyme.

4   Place the tomato rounds on top and season with salt, remaining thyme and basil.

5   Sprinkle remaining olive oil on top and cook in the oven for 15-20 minutes.

Alternative: Once the aubergines and tomatoes are cooked, you might place cheese slices on top, letting the cheese melt slightly for few minutes in the oven before serving.

INGREDIENTS

2 aubergines, peeled in strips and cut into 1 cm rounds

2-3 tbsp olive oil

Freshly ground black pepper, to taste

2 big tomatoes, sliced into 1 cm thick rounds

Salt, to taste

Pinch of thyme, fresh if possible

Pinch of basil, dried

Baked Potatoes with Mushrooms

INGREDIENTS

3 potatoes, cut in 1 cm cubes

2 cups button mushrooms, peeled and cut in half

1 red bell pepper, chopped into 1 cm cubes

1 green bell pepper, chopped into 1 cm cubes

Pinch of salt

½ tsp freshly ground black pepper

1 tsp thyme

Pinch of asafoetida (optional)

½ tsp red chilli powder (optional)

3-4 tbsp olive oil

PREPARATION

1　Preheat the oven to 220°C / 450°F / Gas mark 6.

2　Put potatoes, mushrooms and peppers in a deep oven tray.

3　Add salt, pepper, thyme, asafoetida, chilli powder and olive oil, and mix.

4　Place the tray on the middle shelf of the oven and cook for about 20 minutes.

5　Serve hot.

Cheese Balls

PREPARATION

1 Mix grated cheese, chopped walnuts, olive oil, chilli powder, oregano, dill and parsley or coriander together. Form small round balls.

2 Serve with black olives and cherry tomatoes. You can serve the cheese mixture as a spread on bread or crackers.

INGREDIENTS

2 cups feta cheese, grated

¾ cup walnuts, coarsely chopped

½ cup olive oil

1 tsp red chilli powder

1 tsp dry oregano

2 tbsp fresh dill, finely chopped

1 tbsp fresh parsley or coriander, finely chopped

Black olives

Cherry tomatoes

You're never too old to taste a new dish, try a new recipe, or learn a new habit.

Falafel

INGREDIENTS

1 cup dry chickpeas, soaked overnight with ½ tsp baking soda in the water

1-2 tbsp water

Pinch of asafoetida

1 tsp salt

¼-½ tsp ground black pepper

¼-½ tsp red chilli powder or fresh green chillies, according to taste

1-2 tsp ground cumin

1 tsp ground coriander

½ tsp granulated sugar

¼ tsp turmeric (optional)

3-4 tsp sesame seeds

1 tsp baking powder

Sunflower oil, for frying

PREPARATION

1 Put the soaked and drained chickpeas into a blender or food processor and grind to a paste. If needed, add 1 to 2 tablespoons of water, but not more. Use a spatula to push down the sides every now and again to redistribute the mixture, as it tends to compact around and underneath the blades.

2 Keep processing the mixture until it is smooth.

3 Put the paste in a bowl.

4 If the paste is thin, then add a little chickpea flour.

5 Add all the remaining ingredients, except the oil, and mix well.

6 Place the bowl in the fridge and leave for at least an hour. It can be kept in the fridge for up to two days.

7 Put the oil in a frying pan, about 2 cm deep, and heat for about 10 minutes on a medium heat.

8 To shape the falafel balls, moisten or oil your hands. They should be moist enough so that the mixture does not stick to your hands.

9 Take a tablespoon of the mixture and shape it into a 1 cm to 1.5 cm patty, i.e. a flattened ball. Fry on both sides and serve warm.

Falafels can be eaten with pitta breads, as well as dips such as fava (broad bean dip), cacik or plain home-made yoghurt. See pages 154, 172, 174 and 176.

Mushrooms and Peppers

PREPARATION

1 Peel the mushrooms. Do not wash them. Clean the stems by cutting off the ends. It is important that the mushrooms are dry to retain the flavour while cooking.

2 Heat oil and butter in a pan on a medium heat. Add black pepper and mushrooms and sauté for few minutes, keeping the heat medium to high. Do not add salt at this stage, as this will impair the taste of the mushrooms.

3 Add red and yellow peppers and sauté them for about 3 minutes.

4 Add salt, thyme and oregano. Reduce the heat to low, cover, cook for 5 more minutes and serve.

Alternative: You can add 1 tbsp of tomato paste, a pinch of asafoetida and ½ tsp chilli powder while cooking.

INGREDIENTS

2 cups of button mushrooms

1 tbsp olive oil

1 tbsp butter

½-1 tsp black pepper, coarsely ground

1 yellow pepper, chopped into 1 cm cubes

1 red bell pepper, chopped into 1 cm cubes

½ tsp salt

1 tsp thyme

1 tsp oregano

Fresh coriander, for decoration

To take care in what I eat means to be kind to myself.

Potato Rolls

INGREDIENTS

4 medium potatoes, boiled or steamed

5 tbsp cheddar cheese, coarsely grated

4 tbsp milk

4 tbsp plain flour

½ tsp salt, to taste

½ tsp freshly ground black pepper, to taste

Pinch of red chilli powder (optional)

1 green bell pepper or 2 green chillies, very finely chopped

3 tbsp fresh parsley and dill (or corriander), finely chopped

3 tbsp fine semolina or cornmeal for coating

Oil, for frying

PREPARATION

1 Mash the potatoes. Add grated cheese, milk, flour, salt, pepper, red chilli powder, green pepper, parsley and dill. Mix to a smooth dough texture and form rolls.

2 Coat the rolls with semolina or cornmeal, and fry.

3 Blot the rolls on kitchen paper to remove excess oil.

Alternative: Instead of coating with semolina, you can dip the potato rolls in a chickpea flour batter and deep fry. The batter is made by mixing water with a cupful of chickpea flour. The consistency of the batter should be a little thicker than pancake batter. These rolls are very tasty and can also be served with spicy tomato and red pepper chutney. See page 182.

 The art of cooking is to transform raw ingredients into a delight.

INGREDIENTS

2 cups fine wholewheat flour
  or chapatti flour

½-1 tsp salt

2 tbsp plain yoghurt

3 tbsp oil

¾ cup warm water

Wraps

PREPARATION

1 Mix the flour and salt together in a bowl. Mix in the yoghurt and oil with your fingers until the mixture resembles coarse breadcrumbs. Stir in warm water slowly, so that the dough holds together and work it with your hands.

2 Turn the dough out onto a lightly floured surface, and knead for 2-3 minutes until smooth. Do not overwork it.

3 If sticky, then put a little oil in your palms and knead. Form the dough into a ball.

4 Put a 25 cm non-stick frying pan / flat pan over a medium heat.

5 Place the ball of dough on a lightly floured surface, cut and shape into 6-8 small balls.

6 Dip each ball into flour and use a rolling pin to roll each ball into a circle - as thin as you can - roughly 15 cm in diameter. Whilst rolling, dust flour on top and underneath to ensure that it doesn't stick.

7 When the pan is hot, but not smoking, cook the wrap until slightly puffed out (takes about 20-30 seconds).

8 Turn it over and cook the other side for 20-30 seconds more, or until you see light brown spots on the surface.

9 Place on a cooling rack. Cook the remaining wraps in the same way.

10 Prepare arabiata-type sauce as described on page 134 or a salad filling, or any other filling you can think of.

11 Spread the filling on the wrap and roll it up.

Serve with different dips and salad leaves or cheese slices. Freshly made wraps are soft and delicious at room temperature and, to reheat them, you can warm them briefly in a low oven. They keep well in the fridge, wrapped in paper towels and sealed in a plastic bag, and they also freeze nicely.

Baked Potato Slices
with Cheese Sauce

INGREDIENTS

3 to 4 potatoes, peeled and sliced into 1 cm thick rounds

4 to 5 tbsp olive oil

Salt and ground black pepper, to taste

Pinch of cumin powder

6 tbsp mixture of grated feta cheese and Greek yoghurt

Few drops of chilli tomato sauce (optional)

½ tsp mustard

Pinch of asafoetida (optional)

Dill, very finely chopped (optional)

Red chilli powder, to taste

Red chilli flakes, for decoration

PREPARATION

1　Preheat oven to 220°C / 450°F / Gas mark 6.

2　Place the potato slices on a greased oven tray, sprinkle with olive oil, salt, black pepper and cumin, and cook on the middle shelf of the oven for about 15 minutes.

3　Mix all other ingredients, except the chilli flakes, together to form a cheese sauce.

4　Pour sauce on top of the potato slices, decorate with chilli flakes and serve.

Bird's Nest Potatoes

PREPARATION

1 Mash the potatoes. Add salt, pepper, ground coriander, asafoetida, olive oil and lemon juice. Mix by hand to form a smooth dough.

2 Form the mixture into walnut-sized balls. Use thumb to make a slight hollow on top.

3 Sauté finely grated carrots in sunflower oil for 3 to 4 minutes.

4 Coat each potato ball with finely chopped dill and put yoghurt into the hollows. Decorate by placing sautéed carrots around the yoghurt, sprinkle on red chilli powder and serve.

If any are left over, they can be stored in the fridge.

INGREDIENTS

4 potatoes, boiled or steamed

Salt and ground black pepper, to taste

1 tsp ground coriander

Pinch of asafoetida (optional)

4-5 tbsp olive oil

Juice of ½ lemon

1 carrot, finely grated, for decoration

1 tbsp sunflower oil for sautéing

½ cup finely chopped dill

4 tbsp plain yoghurt

Red chilli powder for decoration

Sprinkle good wishes into everything you cook – and taste the difference.

Egg-less Omelette

INGREDIENTS

1 cup rocket and parsley mixture, washed and finely chopped

1 tbsp chickpea flour (can be replaced with plain flour)

3 tbsp cornmeal

3 tbsp plain yoghurt or Greek yoghurt

3 tbsp water

2-3 tbsp grated cheddar cheese or feta cheese (optional)

Salt and ground black pepper, to taste

1 tbsp butter for frying each omelette

PREPARATION

1 Mix all ingredients, except butter, in a bowl. You might find that the batter is firm, but do not add any more water as the mixture will soften once in the pan.

2 Put 1 tbsp of butter in a shallow frying pan on medium heat. Place the batter on the pan as one big portion or as a few small rounds. Shallow fry both sides of the omelette until crisp and golden.

Serve with salad for a light lunch or as breakfast.

Angels create a welcoming kitchen through love-filled calm.

31

Grilled Cheese on Toast

PREPARATION

1   Mix all the ingredients together and spread on slices of bread.

2   Grill for 5 minutes.

Grilled cheese on toast can be part of a nice extended breakfast or a light lunch, served with salad.

INGREDIENTS

2 tbsp grated cheese (Greek feta or Cheddar cheese)

1 tbsp Greek yoghurt

2 tbsp finely chopped fresh herbs (parsley, coriander and rosemary or any other herb), to taste

¼ tsp chilli powder

Pinch of black pepper

Small pinch of turmeric

2 slices of bread

Okra and Potato Chips

INGREDIENTS

½ kg okras, washed and dried
(no need to cut the tops)

3 to 4 medium size potatoes,
peeled and cut into chips

4 tbsp olive oil

Salt and black pepper, to taste

Alternative:
You can also serve these with
a spicy tomato sauce.

PREPARATION

1 Preheat the oven to 220°C / 450°F / Gas Mark 6.

2 Place the washed, dried okras and potato chips on a greased
baking tray. Sprinkle olive oil, salt and pepper over.

3 Cook in the oven, middle shelf, for about 15 minutes and serve.

You can prepare a sauce by mixing 1 cup of plain yoghurt and 1 heaped
tsp of readymade mustard. This sauce goes together very well.

SPICY TOMATO SAUCE

1 Blend 2-3 fresh tomatoes in a blender with a couple of green
chillies and fresh ginger (peeled, 2 cm approximately).

2 Heat 1 tbsp of oil in a small pan and, when hot, add 1 tsp mustard
seeds and cover. When the mustard seeds have popped, add 1/4
tsp of asafoetida and the blended tomatoes.

3 Also add ½ tsp turmeric powder (optional). Let it cook for a few
minutes for the flavours to release, then add the sauce to the
okra and potato chips.

4 Decorate with fresh coriander and serve with rice.

Spinach in Light Sauce

PREPARATION

1 Steam the spinach until soft (about 5 minutes) or cook with very little water (about ¼ cup) on medium to low heat, covered .

2 Drain the cooked spinach, put onto a plate and cut into small pieces when cool. Do not use the thick stems - you may keep them for soup.

3 Put olive oil or butter into a pan, add the flour and fry for approximately 4 minutes until the mixture is cream in colour. Add in the spinach and mix well.

4 Mix in milk and salt, and cook for about 4-5 minutes, stirring continuously. The milk could be replaced by water.

5 Prepare sauce by mixing plain yoghurt and asafoetida in a bowl. Pour olive oil on top and sprinkle with chilli powder.

6 Turn the spinach onto a plate and serve with sauce.

Alternative: You may place the cooked spinach in light sauce on a serving plate, pour the yoghurt and asafoetida mixture on top and decorate with olive oil and chilli powder.

INGREDIENTS

1 kg spinach, cleaned and washed

½ cup olive oil or 125 gm butter

6 tbsp whole wheat flour, cornmeal or plain flour

1 cup of milk

Pinch of salt

FOR THE SAUCE

1 cup plain yoghurt

Pinch of asafoetida (optional)

1-2 tbsp olive oil

1 tsp red chilli powder

Courgette Délice

INGREDIENTS

3 courgettes, peeled

¼ cup plain flour

¼ cup olive oil

½ cup plain yoghurt

½ cup walnuts, chopped coarsely

Pinch of red chilli powder

Pinch of salt

½ cup fresh dill, finely chopped

Pinch of asafoetida (optional)

Walnuts, for decoration

PREPARATION

1 Steam the courgettes and mash them.

2 Fry the flour in oil in a saucepan. Add the courgettes. Simmer for 2-3 minutes.

3 Mix in the yoghurt, chopped walnuts, chilli powder, salt, chopped dill and asafoetida to form a sauce.

4 Mix courgettes and sauce, decorate with walnuts and serve.

Crisp and fresh green salads with traditional leaf lettuces and young spinach and rocket – combined with lentils, beans and nuts – so many flavours to serve with the various salad vegetables, fresh from the world's garden to mix and dress with subtle flavours.

A tempting accompaniment to a main course or a dish that's tasty and tempting enough as a course on its own. Salads promote health and offer a variety of flavours and textures.

SALADS

Artichoke Salad

INGREDIENTS

2 artichokes

2 tbsp olive oil

1 tbsp lemon juice, freshly squeezed

¼ tsp salt

Pinch of asafoetida (optional)

1 tsp sesame seeds, toasted

1 tbsp fresh dill, finely chopped

PREPARATION

1   Clean the leaves of the artichokes (see page 247). Peel them and soak immediately in water with few drops of lemon juice so they do not turn brown.

2   Place the artichokes in a pan with ½ cup water and few drops of olive oil. Cover and cook on medium heat for about 10 minutes.

3   Mix the sauce ingredients – olive oil, lemon juice, salt and asafoetida (optional).

4   Place the boiled artichokes on serving plate.

5   Pour the sauce on top and decorate with toasted sesame seeds and fresh dill.

Serve with salad leaves.

Beetroot Salad

PREPARATION

1 Boil the beetroots in their skins. Peel and slice about 1 cm thick.

2 For the dressing, mix olive oil, lemon juice or vinegar, salt and asafoetida (optional).

3 Sprinkle ground almonds on top of the beetroot slices.

4 Serve with the dressing.

Alternative: Ready cooked beetroots can also be used to save time.

INGREDIENTS

2-3 beetroots, fresh

2 tbsp olive oil

1 tbsp lemon juice, freshly squeezed, or apple cider vinegar

¼ tsp salt or to taste

Pinch of asafoetida (optional)

Almonds, coarsely ground

Eat freshly cooked food and you will be full of energy.

Cottage Cheese Salad

INGREDIENTS

1 cup cottage cheese

½ green bell pepper, finely chopped

½ red pepper, finely chopped

1 tsp black sesame seeds

1½ tsp oregano

½ tsp thyme

½ tsp red chilli powder

½ cucumber, peeled and diced

2 medium tomatoes, diced

2 tbsp chopped fresh parsley and mint

2-3 green salad leaves, finely chopped

4 tbsp olive oil

PREPARATION

1 Mix all the ingredients together and serve.

2 You can add freshly squeezed lemon juice for a sour taste.

Goes well with cornmeal bread.

As milk and sugar blend well together, let interactions with others also blend in harmony.

Green Salad with Chickpeas

PREPARATION

1 Place the chopped salad leaves in a bowl. Mix in cooked chickpeas and chopped red pepper.

2 For the dressing, mix the olive oil, black pepper, salt and lemon juice, and sprinkle with chilli powder.

3 Pour the dressing over the salad. Add finely chopped herbs, toss and serve.

As a variation, you can add boiled sweetcorn kernels (canned, frozen or fresh) to this salad.

INGREDIENTS

3 cups lettuce leaves, any kind, washed, dried and chopped

1 cup cooked chickpeas (or canned)

1 red bell pepper, chopped

3 to 4 tbsp olive oil

½ tsp ground black pepper

Salt, to taste

1 tbsp lemon juice

1 tsp chilli powder

2 tbsp fresh parsley and mint, finely chopped

The place for stirring things is in the kitchen with a spoon.

Piyaz Bean Salad

INGREDIENTS

2 cups white kidney beans, cooked

3 fresh tomatoes, cut into cubes

1 green bell pepper, finely chopped, or 2 fresh green chilli peppers

1 cup fresh green lettuce leaves, finely chopped

½ cup mixture of fresh dill, parsley and mint, finely chopped

3 to 4 tbsp olive oil

Juice of 1 lemon

1 tsp salt or to taste

1 tsp oregano, dry

1 tsp red chilli powder

Pinch of asafoetida (optional)

PREPARATION

Mix all the ingredients together and serve.

This salad is eaten with burgers and with cacik, as on pages 106, 108 and 172 as a very traditional menu in Turkey.

Rocket Salad with Orange

PREPARATION

1 Put the rocket on a serving plate,

2 Extract the zest and juice from the orange. Sprinkle the orange zest and walnuts on the rocket.

3 To make the dressing, mix the orange juice, olive oil and black pepper, and pour over the leaves.

4 Mix and serve.

INGREDIENTS

2 to 3 cups rocket, washed and dried, (chopped if leaves are large)

1 orange

½ cup walnuts, coarsely chopped

3 tbsp olive oil

Ground black pepper, to taste

Waldorf Salad

INGREDIENTS

3 cups green lettuce leaves
(any variety)

1 Granny Smith apple, cut into
small cubes

1 cup boiled sweetcorn
(fresh or canned)

½ cup walnuts, chopped

½ cup feta cheese, cut into
small cubes

½ cup raisins or sultanas

1-2 tbsp apple cider vinegar,
or to taste

3 tbsp olive oil

3 tbsp chopped parsley

PREPARATION

Mix all the ingredients together and serve.

As you cook, replenish your
energy with the nutrients of
peace and serenity.

Baby Spinach Salad

PREPARATION

Mix all the ingredients together and serve.

INGREDIENTS

3 cups baby spinach, washed, dried and torn by hand

Half a small iceberg lettuce, washed, dried and torn by hand

2 tomatoes, halved and finely sliced

1 medium carrot, finely grated

10 black olives

4 tbsp feta cheese, grated coarsely

2 tbsp finely chopped fresh parsley and mint

3 tbsp olive oil

Celeriac Salad

INGREDIENTS

2 celeriac, peeled, washed and grated coarsely

1 Granny Smith apple, chopped finely

1 cup Greek yoghurt

½ cup walnuts, chopped coarsely

2 tbsp fresh parsley, chopped finely

1 tbsp of apple cider vinegar

2 tbsp olive oil

Pinch of asafoetida (optional)

PREPARATION

Mix all the ingredients together and serve.

Alternative: You can add 2 tbsp of mayonnaise as seen on page 170

Green Lentil and Rice Salad

PREPARATION

1. Put the lentils in a pan; add water, cover to a depth of 2 cm and boil. Add water as required until cooked according to type of lentil used.

2. Drain off the excess water and put lentils in a bowl.

3. Boil the rice separately, initially adding 1 cup of water and adding more as required until cooked.

4. Drain the excess water and add to the bowl with the lentils.

5. Add all the remaining ingredients to the bowl, mix together and serve.

INGREDIENTS

1 cup green or brown lentils

½ cup rice

4 tbsp olive oil

1 green bell pepper, cut in small cubes

1 medium carrot, finely grated

2 tbsp fresh mint, finely chopped

2 tbsp fresh parsley or coriander, finely chopped

1 tsp oregano, dry

½ tsp cumin powder

Salt and freshly ground black pepper, to taste

Juice of 1 lemon

A kitchen is like a laboratory where I can observe many positive qualities within myself.

Rice Salad

INGREDIENTS

1 cup jasmine rice, or any
  other kind of rice, boiled and
  drained

2 medium carrots, boiled and
  cut into pea-sized cubes

½ cup boiled sweetcorn
  (canned or frozen)

½ cup green peas, cooked

½ cup capers (optional)

2 tbsp fresh dill, finely chopped

2 tbsp fresh mint, finely
  chopped

2 tbsp fresh parsley or
  coriander, finely chopped

½ tsp black pepper, freshly
  ground

Salt to taste

Juice of one lemon

3-4 tbsp olive oil

PREPARATION

Mix all the ingredients together and serve.

Nature is the best cook – sometimes eat food just as She offers it.

Russian Salad

PREPARATION

1 Dice the cooked potatoes and carrots into 1 cm cubes, and put into a bowl.

2 Add boiled peas, capers, chopped parsley and/or dill and mayonnaise. Add asafoetida, salt and pepper.

3 Mix with a spoon.

4 Chill in the fridge for about 10 minutes before serving.

INGREDIENTS

4 potatoes, boiled or steamed

2 carrots, boiled or steamed

½ cup boiled peas

½ cup capers

2 tbsp finely chopped parsley and/or dill (optional)

Pinch of asafoetida (optional)

Salt and black pepper to taste

¾ to 1 cup mayonnaise prepared as described on page 170

Attitude flavours food — so choose the mood you want to serve.

A word to cover so many flavours and textures: soup can be an interesting appetiser before the main course, a quick and nutritious snack (home-made soup with fresh ingredients is 'fast food' that's healthy too) or, accompanied by bread, it makes a satisfying supper.

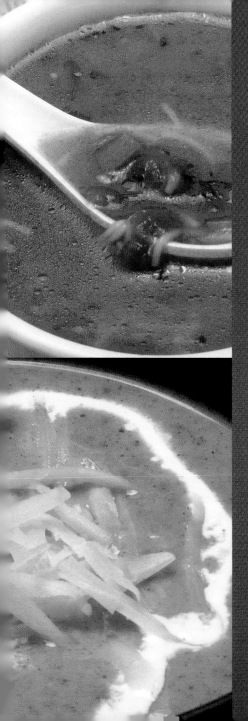

SOUPS

Aubergine and Potato Soup

INGREDIENTS

3 medium potatoes, boiled or
steamed

2½ cups water

1 cup milk

Pinch of cumin powder

¼ tsp ginger powder

1 tsp salt, or to taste

½ tsp black pepper, or to taste

1 medium aubergine, peeled

½ tbsp butter

1 tsp dried oregano

½ tsp chilli powder

PREPARATION

1 Blend the cooked potatoes with water and milk in a pan using a
hand blender.

2 Add cumin powder, ginger powder, salt and black pepper. Place
on medium heat and bring to the boil.

3 Cut the peeled aubergine into 4 lengthwise and chop into
pieces 2 cm long.

4 Heat butter into a small pan, add chopped aubergine, oregano
and chilli powder. Fry for about 5 minutes on medium heat
until the aubergine is soft and golden.

5 Add the fried aubergine to the potato mix and cover. Leave for
5 to 10 minutes and serve.

For variety you can add boiled red lentils, if preferred, at the time
of blending the potatoes.

This is a delicious rich flavoured soup.

Minestrone Soup

PREPARATION

1   Put all the ingredients, except the fresh herbs, into a large pot.

2   Add water, bring to boil, and then simmer.

3   When cooked, add the fresh herbs and serve.

You can adjust the vegetable combination according to your own taste and create your own version of minestrone.

INGREDIENTS

2 tbsp potatoes, peeled and finely diced

1 cup broccoli, cut into small pieces

½ cup cauliflower, cut into small pieces

2 carrots, peeled and finely diced

½ cup kidney beans, cooked

3 tbsp olive oil

2 tbsp tomato purée

1 tsp salt and ½ tsp fresh ground black pepper, to taste

4 cups water

2 tbsp fresh parsley, mint and dill mixture (optional), finely chopped

Spices are like the pleasures of life – a pinch is interesting, too much is indigestible.

Broccoli Soup with Croutons

INGREDIENTS

2 cups broccoli, finely chopped

3 potatoes, diced

4 cups water

1 cup milk or soya milk

Salt and ground black pepper,
   to taste

2 tbsp olive oil or 1 tbsp butter

PREPARATION

1   Cook the broccoli and potatoes in the water and milk.

2   Use a blender to blend the vegetables in the pot.

3   Add salt, black pepper and olive oil or butter.

CROUTONS

Fry day-old cubes of bread of about 2 cm square in a little olive oil or butter until golden.

Serve soup sprinkled with croutons.

Stir patience into all you prepare.

Chickpea and Yoghurt Soup

PREPARATION

1 Heat the water in a pan.

2 Mix the flour and plain yoghurt in a bowl until smooth. Take one cup of warm water from the pan, add to the flour and yoghurt; mix until smooth.

3 Return the mixture to the pan of warm water, add salt and stir constantly on medium heat for about 10 minutes.

4 Add the chickpeas. Stir constantly until it comes to boil, then turn off the heat.

5 Put the butter, dried mint, red chilli powder and asafoetida into a separate small pan and melt.

6 Pour the butter onto the soup and serve.

INGREDIENTS

4-5 cups water

3 tbsp plain flour or chickpea flour

2 tbsp plain yoghurt

Salt, to taste

1 cup chickpeas, boiled

1 tbsp butter

1 tbsp dried mint

1 tsp red chilli powder

Pinch of asafoetida (optional)

Love and thoughtfulness transforms plain food into a banquet.

Hot and Sour Soup

INGREDIENTS

2 tbsp olive oil

2 tbsp fresh green beans, finely chopped (about 1 cm)

1 tbsp mushrooms, finely chopped

½ cup cabbage, finely chopped

½ cup carrots, very finely chopped

½ tsp red chilli powder, or to taste

2 tsp soy sauce, to taste

1 tbsp tomato purée

1 tbsp sugar

1 tbsp cider vinegar

1 tsp salt, to taste

3-4 cups water

1 tbsp cornflour or rice flour, for a thicker consistency (optional)

PREPARATION

1 Heat the oil in a pan and sauté the green beans and mushrooms.

2 Add cabbage and carrots and sauté for 2 more minutes.

3 Add all the other ingredients and bring to the boil. Simmer for 5 minutes and serve.

4 For a thicker consistency, mix 1 tbsp of cornflour or rice flour with ½ cup of soup stock and return it to the pan. Simmer for few more minutes.

5 Serve hot.

Cream Tomato Soup

PREPARATION

1 Blend the tomatoes using a blender.

2 Put the olive oil or butter and flour in a pan and fry for 2-3 minutes.

3 Add the tomatoes first and mix with a hand, whisk to ensure a smooth consistency, and then add tomato purée, sugar, salt and pepper to the pan. Add water and bring to boil.

4 Add the cream and simmer for 2-3 minutes (save 1 tbsp of cream for decoration).

5 Decorate with finely chopped parsley and a swirl of cream and grated cheese.

6 Serve hot.

INGREDIENTS

5 medium sized fresh tomatoes, cut coarsely

2 tbsp olive oil or 1 tbsp butter

2 tbsp plain flour

2 tbsp tomato purée

1 tsp sugar

Salt and ground black pepper, to taste

4 cups water

¾ cup single cream

1 tbsp fresh chopped parsley (optional)

Grated cheese, for decoration (optional)

Vermicelli Soup

INGREDIENTS

2 tbsp olive oil

1 green pepper, finely chopped

Salt and black pepper, to taste

Pinch of asafoetida (optional)

1 cup fresh or canned
   tomatoes, diced into cubes

½ cup vermicelli, crushed

6 cups water

1 tbsp butter

3 tbsp fresh parsley, chopped

PREPARATION

1 Put the oil into a pan on a high heat. Add the chopped green
   pepper, salt, black pepper and asafoetida, and sauté for a few
   minutes.

2 Add the tomato cubes and reduce the heat to medium. Cover
   and boil for 1-2 minutes.

3 Add the vermicelli, water and butter. Boil, until the vermicelli is
   soft, about 6-8 minutes, stirring from time to time.

4 Remove soup from the heat, add fresh parsley and leave to
   stand for 5 minutes before serving.

You can increase the quantity of vermicelli if you prefer a thicker
soup.

To cook means to care, to bake means to bestow.

Courgette Soup with Dill

PREPARATION

1 Wash the courgettes, cut each one into 4-5 pieces and boil with 2 cups of water.

2 Purée the boiled courgettes and return to the pot. Add the remaining water, milk, cumin, ginger, salt and pepper to taste and bring to the boil.

3 Add cream and simmer for 2-3 minutes.

4 Add freshly chopped dill and stir. Serve hot.

5 You can decorate with dry roasted cumin seeds before serving.

You can add one peeled, chopped potato to the courgettes as they cook, if you wish to have a thicker consistency.

INGREDIENTS

5 medium courgettes

3 cups water

1 cup milk or soya milk

½ tsp ground cumin

A pinch of ground ginger, to taste

Salt and ground black pepper, to taste

⅓ cup single cream

3 tbsp fresh dill, chopped finely

Dry roasted cumin seed (optional)

Sometimes, eat in silence – and savour the taste and the effect.

Cauliflower Soup with Mushrooms

INGREDIENTS

2 cups cauliflower, chopped into small florets

3 cups water

1 cup milk or soya milk

5 or 6 mushrooms, peeled and sliced medium to thick

1 tbsp olive or sunflower oil

¼ tsp black pepper, or to taste

¼ tsp ground cumin

Salt, to taste

1 tbsp freshly chopped coriander (optional)

1 tbsp freshly chopped parsley (optional)

Chilli flakes for decoration

PREPARATION

1   Steam the cauliflower until very soft. Put the cauliflower into a pan, add 2 cups of water and blend with hand blender.

2   Add 1 cup of milk or soya milk to the mixture and place on medium heat.

3   Peel the mushrooms (ensure they are dry, as this affects the taste). Slice and put in a separate pan with 1 tbsp olive oil or butter and fry on a high heat until golden.

4   Add the fried mushrooms to the cauliflower, adding black pepper, cumin and salt. Bring to the boil and turn the heat off immediately.

5   Add the fresh herbs, chilli flakes and serve.

Carrot Soup with Coriander

PREPARATION

1 Put olive oil or butter into a pan, sauté the carrots, grated ginger and ground coriander for 3-4 minutes. Add water and cook until the carrots are soft.

2 Place 2 tbsp of cornflour in a bowl, add 5 to 6 tbsp of stock (taken from the soup) and mix with a hand whisk. Pour this mixture back into the pan and stir for a few minutes.

3 This will thicken the soup - you can omit this if you prefer a thin soup.

4 Add salt, pepper and chopped fresh coriander, simmer for a few minutes more and serve hot.

INGREDIENTS

2 tbsp olive oil or 1 tbsp butter

6 carrots, diced into ½ cm cubes

1 tsp fresh ginger, grated

1-2 tsp dry coriander, ground

4 cups water

2 tbsp cornflour

Salt and ground black pepper, to taste

2-3 tbsp fresh coriander, chopped finely

Be creative in the kitchen: sometimes follow the recipe, and sometimes follow your heart.

Kale Soup with White Sauce

INGREDIENTS

4 cups chopped kale, including stems if tender

6 cups water

½ tsp bicarbonate of soda

2 tbsp olive oil or butter

½ cup cracked bulgar wheat

¾ cup sweetcorn

1 cup black-eyed beans, cooked

1 tsp salt and coarsely ground black pepper, or to taste

4 tbsp plain yoghurt

2 tbsp cornmeal

PREPARATION

1   Boil the chopped kale with 4 cups water and ½ tsp bicarbonate of soda (this keeps the colour of the kale bright green).

2   Add remaining 2 cups of water, olive oil or butter, bulgar wheat, sweetcorn, black-eyed beans, salt and pepper, and boil for 10 more minutes.

3   Mix the yogurt and cornmeal in a separate bowl, slowly add about 1 cup of the soup stock taken from the pan and mix until smooth. Pour this mixture back into the soup pan, boil for a further 5 to 10 minutes and serve hot.

NOTES

You can use rice or couscous instead of bulgur wheat, and spinach instead of kale.

Adjust the quantity of black pepper, oil or butter and salt according to taste.

Mushroom Soup

PREPARATION

1 Warm the olive oil or butter in a pan. Add mushrooms and black pepper, and fry for 2 minutes.

2 Add the water, salt and milk, and bring to the boil.

3 In a small bowl, place the cornmeal. Add ½ cup of the stock from the above mixture and mix with a fork or a hand whisk.

4 Pour this mixture back into the soup and stir. Let it boil for a few minutes.

5 Simmer for 2 more minutes and add fresh herbs.

6 Serve with croutons (optional).

CROUTONS

1 Fry day-old 2 cm sized cubes of bread in a little butter until golden.

2 Sprinkle croutons onto soup and serve.

INGREDIENTS

2 tbsp olive oil or 1 tbsp butter

20 button mushrooms, peeled and sliced

Salt and ground black pepper, to taste

4 cups water

1 cup milk or soya milk

1 tbsp cornmeal

1 tbsp chopped fresh parsley and dill mixture, or any other fresh herb

The range of recipes that follows in this section amply shows the breadth of vegetarian variety – a vast spread of vegetables, grains and pulses.

Freshly picked, selected ingredients, and an exotic choice of herbs and spices (see page 246 to 251) are available to the discerning and imaginative vegetarian cook.

Many have been attracted to vegetarian cuisine by the unexpected variety of taste experiences and subtle flavours.

MAIN DISHES & ACCOMPANIMENTS

INGREDIENTS

2 tbsp olive oil

1 green bell pepper chopped finely

1 carrot, shredded finely

1 cup soya mince, dry

½ tbsp salt

½ tbsp ground black pepper

½ tsp thyme

1 tsp chilli powder

Pinch of ground cumin to taste

Pinch of asafoetida (optional)

⅓ to ½ cup hot water

25 Brussels sprouts

1 cup rocket leaves, chopped fine

1 tbsp ground flax seeds, soaked in few tbsp of hot water

Brussels Sprouts with Mince Balls

2 to 3 tbsp tomato paste

Oil, for deep frying

2-3 tbsp additional tomato paste (for the sauce)

1 cup warm water (for the sauce)

PREPARATION

1 Place the oil in a pan, put on medium to high heat. Add the chopped green pepper and sauté for a few minutes.

2 Add the shredded carrots, sauté for 1 to 2 minutes more, add the dry soya mince, salt and pepper, thyme, chilli powder, cumin, pinch of asafoetida, and mix.

3 Let the mixture stay for few minutes on the heat. Add ⅓ to ½ cup hot water to the mixture and cover with a lid, bring the heat to very low and simmer for 5 to 10 minutes.

4 Place the Brussels sprouts in the steamer or cook them with a little oil and very little water, cover with a lid and cook on low heat. Add salt and pepper to taste.

5 Place the cooked soya mince mixture into a bowl. Add finely chopped rocket leaves, soaked flax seeds powder and 2 to 3 tbs tomato paste and form dough.

6 Make small balls and deep fry them. Place on a plate covered with paper towel to remove excess oil.

7 In a pan, mix 2 to 3 tbsp of tomato paste with 1 cup warm water. Add Brussels sprouts and deep fried balls, simmer for 5 to 10 minutes and serve.

Celeriac in Olive Oil

PREPARATION

1 Heat the oil in a pan. Add green chillies or peppers and black pepper, and sauté for a couple of minutes.

2 Add carrot rounds, potato slices and celeriac slices, and sauté for a few more minutes.

3 Stir in lemon juice or quince, salt and sugar.

4 Lower the temperature and add a very small splash of hot water to start with. Cover and cook for 15-20 minutes on a low heat.

5 Check from time to time whether the dish needs water. If so, add hot water in very small quantities. Check that all the vegetables are cooked properly before turning off the heat.

6 Decorate with fresh herbs and serve warm.

This is a very typical dish from Turkey that goes well with plain rice and yoghurt.

INGREDIENTS

3 to 4 tbsp olive oil

2 fresh green chillies or 1 green bell pepper, chopped into about 2 cm sized pieces

Ground black pepper, to taste (optional)

2 carrots, sliced in 1 cm thick rounds

2 medium sized potatoes, halved and sliced in D shape, 1 cm thick

1 large or 2 medium celeriac, sliced in D shape, 1 cm thick

½ fresh lemon juice or 1 quince, peeled and diced

1 tsp salt or to taste

½ cup hot water

½ tsp granulated sugar

2 tbsp dill and fresh parsley finely chopped

Cracked Bulgar Wheat with Red Kidney Beans

INGREDIENTS

3-4 tbsp olive oil

3 green chillies or 1 green bell pepper, chopped finely

2-3 fresh tomatoes, peeled and cut into cubes, or 1 cup of canned tomatoes

1 cup red kidney beans, boiled

1 cup cracked bulgar wheat, washed and drained

½ tsp salt and ½ tsp ground black pepper, or to taste

½ tsp red chilli powder, to taste (optional)

Water, enough to cover the cracked wheat, boiling

1 tbsp of tomato paste

3 tbsp fresh dill and mint, finely chopped (optional)

1 tbsp fresh parsley, finely chopped (optional)

PREPARATION

1 Heat the olive oil in a pan, on medium to high heat.

2 Add chopped chillies or pepper and sauté for few minutes.

3 Add tomatoes, boiled red kidney beans, tomato paste, salt, pepper and red chilli powder. Cover, bring heat to medium and cook for 5 minutes.

4 Add cracked wheat and enough water to cover the mixture. Cover and cook on medium heat.

5 Keep boiled water aside and check the cracked wheat from time to time. Add water, only if necessary, in small quantities, making sure the mixture does not stick at the bottom.

6 When the cracked wheat is cooked, turn off the heat and let it rest for 15 minutes.

It can be served with plain yoghurt.

Plain food elegantly served looks like a banquet and tastes like a feast.

Fancy Rice Burgers

PREPARATION

1 In a bowl, mix together lentils, rice, walnuts, Greek yoghurt (or ground linseed and water mixture), salt, black pepper and finely chopped fresh parsley or coriander. Form large flat oval-shaped burgers.

2 In another bowl, mix the flour with water and form a batter. The consistency should be like pancake batter.

3 According to your taste, spices can be added to this batter, such as asafoetida, cumin powder, chilli powder or green chillies.

4 Pour the oil into a pan and heat on medium to high heat.

5 Coat the burgers with the batter and shallow fry them until golden.

6 Put the cooked burgers onto a paper towel to remove excess oil. Serve hot or warm.

Alternative: You can use hazelnuts or sunflower seeds as a substitute for walnuts, or a mixture of them, or any other nuts, according to your taste and availability.

INGREDIENTS

1 cup green or brown lentils, boiled

1 cup rice, boiled

½ cup walnuts, chopped coarsely

1 tbsp Greek yoghurt or 1 tbsp ground linseed mixed with 3 tbsp hot water

1 tsp salt and 1 tsp black pepper, or to taste

2 tbsp fresh parsley or coriander, chopped finely

½ cup chickpea (gram) flour or plain white flour, for batter

1½ cups water for batter

Sunflower oil, for shallow frying

Fresh Tomato and Green Bean Rice

INGREDIENTS

4 tbsp olive oil

3 cups (½ kg) fresh green beans, chopped 1 cm long

1 tsp salt and ½ tsp pepper, or to taste

3 medium fresh tomatoes, shredded coarsely

1 cup rice

1 cup hot water

PREPARATION

1 Put the olive oil into a pan and sauté the chopped beans for couple of minutes on a high heat. Add salt and pepper.

2 Cover, lower the heat to medium and cook for 5 minutes.

3 Add shredded fresh tomato, rice and hot water (enough to cover rice). Cover and cook for around 15 minutes.

4 Check if rice requires additional water and, if necessary, add hot water in small quantities until the rice is cooked.

5 Turn off the heat and let the rice stand for about 10-15 minutes before serving.

You can serve this rice together with plain yoghurt as a light meal or together with the falafel-type burgers. See page 140.

Green Beans in Tomato Sauce

PREPARATION

1 Heat the oil in a pan.

2 Add tomatoes and sauté them for couple of minutes.

3 Add green beans and sauté for couple of minutes more .

4 Add salt, pepper and sugar.

5 Reduce the heat to low, cover and cook for 20 minutes stirring occasionally.

This is a very typical Turkish summer dish usually prepared with stringless beans.

You can serve it with fresh bread and/or rice and plain yoghurt.

INGREDIENTS

4 tbsp olive oil

3-4 fresh tomatoes, diced, or 1 cup chopped tinned tomatoes

½ kg fresh green beans, washed and cut into 4 cm length

1 tsp salt, or to taste

½ tsp fresh black pepper, coarsely ground, or to taste

1 tsp sugar

Lentil Burgers

INGREDIENTS

2-3 green chillies or 1 green bell pepper, chopped very finely

3 tbsp olive oil or sunflower oil

2 medium tomatoes cut into cubes

1 tsp salt and 1 tsp black pepper, or to taste

2 cups green or brown lentils, boiled

2 tbsp cornmeal + ½ cup fine semolina + 2 tbsp chickpea (gram) flour

1 tsp cumin

3 tbsp finely chopped parsley or coriander

Additional cornmeal, to coat the burgers

Sunflower oil, for shallow frying

PREPARATION

1   Sauté the chillies or pepper in olive or sunflower oil for 2-3 minutes. Add the tomatoes, salt and black pepper, and cook for a further 3 minutes on a high heat.

2   Add the cooked lentils, cover and cook for about 10 minutes on medium heat.

3   Allow the mixture to cool down, then mix in the cornmeal, semolina, chickpea flour, cumin, chopped parsley or coriander and form a dough. Add more chickpea flour if needed.

4   Shape into burgers.

5   Coat the burgers with cornmeal. Shallow fry both sides in a frying pan using sunflower oil, on a medium to high heat.

6   Put the cooked burgers onto a paper towel to remove excess oil. Serve hot or warm.

Serve with rice and/or salad.

Oriental Burgers

PREPARATION

1. Mash the potatoes in a bowl. Add salt, thyme, cumin and semolina, and mix together. The potatoes should be warm to soften the semolina. Cover and leave the mixture to rest for about 10 minutes.

2. Place butter, sliced mushrooms, black pepper and asafoetida in a pan on a high heat. Ensure the mushrooms are dry and do not add any salt at this stage as it would cause the mushrooms to release water.

3. Sauté mushrooms for 5 to 7 minutes, until they turn brown.

4. Add mushrooms and chopped fresh parsley to the potato mixture, and salt to taste. Mix well and form burgers. Coat each burger with plain or chickpea flour.

5. Pour some sunflower oil in a pan and shallow fry both sides of each burger, turning a few times.

6. Put the cooked burgers onto a paper towel to remove excess oil. Serve hot or warm.

Serve with mixed salad.

INGREDIENTS

3 medium potatoes, peeled, then steamed or boiled

½ tsp salt, or to taste

1 tsp thyme

1 tsp cumin

½ cup fine semolina

2 tbsp butter

16 button mushrooms, peeled and medium sliced

1 tsp black pepper

Pinch of asafoetida (optional)

3 tbsp fresh parsley, chopped finely

½ cup plain flour or chickpea (gram) flour, for coating the burgers

Sunflower oil, for shallow frying

Fennel and Potato Stir-fry with Peanuts

INGREDIENTS

3-4 tbsp sunflower oil

1 tsp mustard seeds

½ tsp asafoetida

2-3 tbsp peanuts

2 fennel roots, cut into 4 cm lengths and 1 cm thick

2-3 green chillies, finely chopped (optional)

2 potatoes cut lengthways into 1 cm thick chips

5-6 tbsp chickpea (gram) flour, roasted in 2 tbsp of oil for 2 minutes

1-2 tsp ground cumin and coriander seed mix

2 tbsp lemon juice

1-2 tbsp fresh coriander, finely chopped

PREPARATION

1   Heat the oil in a medium-sized pan. When it is hot, add the mustard seeds and cover.

2   After the seeds have popped, add asafoetida and cook for a few seconds. Add the peanuts and fry for a minute, then add the chopped fennel.

3   Stir the mixture, allowing the fennel to cook for a couple of minutes. Add chillies and chopped potatoes, stir everything together, cover and turn the heat to low.

4   Allow to cook, stirring occasionally, until the potatoes are cooked, adding 1 tbsp of water if necessary.

5   Add the roasted chickpea (gram) flour, stir, cover and allow the chickpea flour to cook for a couple of minutes, still on a low heat and stirring occasionally to make sure nothing sticks at the bottom. Then add the ground cumin and coriander seed mix.

6   Remove from heat, add lemon juice and sprinkle with freshly chopped coriander and serve.

This can be served either hot or cold. It can be eaten with the wraps see page 24 or to fill pitta bread see page 154.

111

Beans in a Piquant Sauce

PREPARATION

1   Mix flour, yoghurt, water and cider vinegar in a bowl. Set aside.

2   Put the olive oil into a pan. Add beans, red chilli powder, oregano and salt. Sauté the beans for couple of minutes on medium to high heat.

3   Add the yoghurt sauce and ½ tbsp butter to the beans. Reduce the heat to low, cover and cook for about 10 minutes.

Serve warm, with simple white rice and plain yoghurt or fresh bread.

INGREDIENTS

3 tbsp plain flour

1 tbsp plain yoghurt

½ cup water

4 tbsp cider vinegar

3 tbsp olive oil

3 cups white kidney beans, cooked

½ tsp red chilli powder, or to taste

1 tsp dried oregano

1 tsp salt, or to taste

½ tbsp butter

Wasting food is a sign of wasteful thoughts.

Pasta with Cauliflower and Mushrooms

INGREDIENTS

1 small cauliflower, washed and cut into small bite-sized pieces

Water for steaming cauliflower pieces

Water for boiling pasta

1 tsp salt

2 cups orecchiette or farfalle pasta

¼ cup olive oil

10-12 mushrooms, peeled and quartered

1 tsp black pepper, or to taste

Pinch of asafoetida (optional)

3 tbsp fresh parsley leaves, finely chopped

½ tsp red chilli flakes

PREPARATION

1   Steam the cauliflower pieces until soft.

2   Bring water to the boil in a large saucepan. Add pasta, salt and a few drops of oil to the boiling water and cook until almost, but not quite totally, soft – 'al dente' (9–12 minutes or according to the instructions on the packet) and drain.

3   Heat oil in a large casserole dish over a medium heat, add mushrooms, black pepper and asafoetida. Cook for 5 minutes.

4   Add in pasta and cauliflower, stir over medium heat and cook for few more minutes. Mix in the red chilli flakes and chopped parsley.

Serve with salad and grated cheese.

Red Cabbage with Parsley

PREPARATION

1 Heat oil in a large pan over low-medium heat. Add cumin seeds, wait for few seconds then add red bell pepper and cook until tender.

2 Add cabbage, apple, vinegar, honey and salt. Cover pan and cook over a low heat, stirring occasionally, until the cabbage is soft but not mushy.

3 Turn off heat, add chopped walnuts and fresh parsley, allow to sit for 5 to 10 minutes before serving.

Delicious warm or cold.

INGREDIENTS

2 tbsp olive oil

½ tsp cumin seeds

1 red bell pepper, finely sliced, similar to the cabbage

1 small red cabbage, quartered, cored and very thinly sliced

1 large Granny Smith apple, cored and chopped small

3 tbsp cider vinegar

2 tbsp honey

1 tsp salt

3 tbsp walnuts, coarsely chopped

2 tbsp fresh parsley, finely chopped

Pure ingredients and a thoughtful heart – that's the recipe for respect.

Spinach with Pine Nuts and Raisins

INGREDIENTS

2 tbsp raisins

3 tbsp olive oil

Pinch of asafoetida (optional)

2 bunches spinach, washed and trimmed

3 tbsp pine nuts, roasted

1 tbsp fresh lemon juice

Thin strips of lemon zest, for decoration (optional)

Salt and freshly ground pepper, to taste

PREPARATION

1 Soak raisins in a bowl of cold water for 10 minutes; drain and set aside.

2 Heat olive oil in a large skillet over medium heat. Add asafoetida. After a few seconds, add spinach and cook, stirring, for 1 minute. Cook until spinach leaves are wilted.

3 Add pine nuts, lemon juice, lemon zest and raisins. Season to taste with salt and freshly ground black pepper. Serve.

Alternative: You can replace pine nuts with cashew nuts, hazelnuts or peanuts.

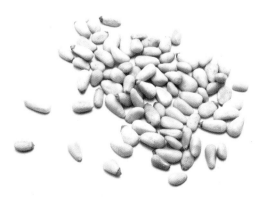

Tagliatelle with Walnuts and Cheese

PREPARATION

1 Bring water to the boil in a large saucepan. Add a few drops of oil, tagliatelle and cook for 10 minutes or according to the instructions on the packet.

2 Drain and return the tagliatelle to the pan. Add the butter, salt and pepper, and mix together.

3 Remove from heat. Add cheese, walnuts and fresh herbs. Mix and serve.

Alternative: Any variety of pasta can be used.

INGREDIENTS

Water, for boiling pasta

Few drops of olive oil

250 gms tagliatelle pasta

2 tbsp butter

½ tsp salt and ½ tsp black pepper, to taste

1 cup feta cheese, coarsely grated

1 cup walnuts, coarsely chopped

½ cup finely chopped fresh parsley or coriander (or any other fresh herb)

Spend quiet time while working in the kitchen and you will get to know and appreciate yourself more.

Kale Stew

INGREDIENTS

3 tbsp olive oil

½ tsp black pepper, coarsely ground, to taste

3 green chillies or 1 green bell pepper, chopped small

1 carrot, cut into small cubes

2 potatoes, diced into small cubes

4 cups kale, chopped

⅓ cup rice

1 tsp salt, or to taste

⅓ tsp bicarbonate of soda

½ cup water, hot

PREPARATION

1 Heat the oil in a pan, add black pepper and chopped green chillies or pepper and sauté for couple of minutes.

2 Add in carrots and potatoes, sauté for a couple of minutes more.

3 Add kale, rice, salt and bicarbonate of soda. Stir and turn the heat low. The bicarbonate of soda helps to keep the kale a bright green colour.

4 Cover and cook for 15 minutes. Check if the rice is cooked (when pressed between your fingers the rice should break).

5 Add a little hot water if necessary, to allow the rice to cook further. Turn off the heat.

6 Serve with yoghurt.

Alternative: You can use Swiss chard or spinach instead of kale for this recipe.

Green Cabbage and Apple Sauté

PREPARATION

1 Heat the oil in a large sauté pan, add asafoetida, salt, pepper and sugar. Add and sauté the cabbage until translucent and it begins to brown.

2 Add apple slices and sauté for a few more minutes or until sizzling.

3 Add a dash of vinegar, mix, cover and turn off heat.

4 Adjust seasoning, add coarsely chopped walnuts and serve. It is delicious hot, warm or at room temperature.

INGREDIENTS

2 tbsp olive oil

Pinch of asafoetida (optional)

Salt and pepper

½ tsp sugar

1 medium green cabbage, quartered, cored and very thinly sliced

1 large crisp, sweet apple, cored and very thinly sliced

1 tbsp apple cider vinegar

1-2 tbsp walnuts, coarsely chopped

Instead of stirring up feelings and getting in a stew – serve a plate of peacefulness.

Quick Tomato Cheese Stew

INGREDIENTS

3 tbsp olive oil

2 green chillies or 1 green bell pepper, chopped

½ red bell pepper, chopped

3 fresh tomatoes, cut into slices

¼ tsp salt and ¼ tsp ground black pepper, or to taste

4-5 slices of Cheddar cheese or feta cheese

1-2 tbsp fresh herbs (parsley, basil or fresh mint, according to taste)

PREPARATION

1 Heat olive oil in a pan and sauté chillies or green pepper and red peppers for couple of minutes.

2 Add tomato slices, salt and black pepper.

3 Cover, turn the heat down to medium and cook for 5 to 7 minutes.

4 Uncover and put cheese slices and fresh herbs on top.

5 Cover and cook for 2 to 3 minutes more then turn off the heat.

6 Leave for 5 minutes until the cheese has melted.

7 Serve with bread.

This is a tasty and very quick recipe.

Artichokes in Olive Oil

PREPARATION

1 Heat the oil in a pan. Add black pepper, boiled green peas, carrot and potato cubes, and sauté for couple of minutes.

2 Add artichokes and salt, and sauté for couple of minutes more.

3 Lower the heat, cover and cook for 15-20 minutes. Check and stir from time to time, adding very little hot water only if necessary (vegetables taste better when cooked on a low heat in steam).

4 Decorate with fresh herbs. Can be served warm or cold.

A typical Turkish/Mediterranean meal and a healthy one, as artichokes are known to help rejuvenate the liver when consumed fresh in season.

INGREDIENTS

3 tbsp olive oil

½ tsp fresh black pepper, coarsely ground

¾ cup green peas, boiled (fresh or frozen)

2 carrots, cut into 1 cm cubes

3 medium potatoes, cut into 1 cm cubes

4 artichokes, cleaned and kept in water with lemon juice to prevent them turning brown

1 tsp salt, or to taste

½ cup water, hot

2 tbsp finely chopped dill and fresh parsley mixture

 A pinch of humour can lighten any situation.

Celeriac in White Sauce

INGREDIENTS

4 tbsp olive oil

2 medium celeriac, peeled and diced

2 medium potatoes, peeled and diced

2 medium carrots, peeled and diced

1½ cup green peas, boiled (fresh or frozen)

1 tsp salt and ¼ tsp freshly ground black pepper, or to taste

3 tbsp plain flour

1 cup water

½ fresh lemon juice, or to taste

2 tbsp fresh parsley, finely chopped

PREPARATION

1 Heat the oil in a pan. Add diced celeriac, potato and carrot and sauté for couple of minutes on a high heat.

2 Add boiled peas, salt and pepper. Reduce the heat to low and cover.

3 Allow the vegetables to cook in their own liquid, as this will result in tastier vegetables. Add a little hot water only if necessary. Avoid lifting the lid too often. The vegetables will cook in about 15 minutes.

4 Mix flour, water and fresh lemon juice in a bowl. Add this sauce to the vegetables, cover and cook for about 5 minutes more on a low heat. Remove from the heat, add chopped parsley.

5 Cover and leave for 5 minutes before serving.

Alternative: You can replace the celeriac with swede if you prefer.

The fresher the food, the more you can enjoy the taste of field and orchard.

Aubergine Pepper Stew

PREPARATION

1 Soak the chopped aubergine in salty water for 5 to 10 minutes. Squeeze out the water (to take away the bitterness of the aubergine).

2 Heat 3-4 tbsp olive oil in a pan, on medium to high heat.

3 Add asafoetida. After a few seconds, add peppers and sauté them for couple of minutes.

4 Add chopped aubergines, tomatoes, cider vinegar, sugar, salt and pepper. (Remember the aubergine will be slightly salty already.)

5 Reduce the heat to low and cover. Cook for about 15 minutes.

6 Drizzle 1-2 tbsp of olive oil on top after cooking (optional).

7 Serve warm or cold.

This is a typical sweet-sour aubergine dish from Turkish/ Mediterranean cuisine that can be served as a light lunch with bread and plain yoghurt, or with plain rice.

INGREDIENTS

2 medium aubergines, peeled (optional) and cut into 2 cm cubes

3-4 tbsp olive oil

Pinch of asafoetida (optional)

1 green and 1 red bell pepper, chopped into 2 cm squares

2 to 3 fresh tomatoes, cut into cubes or 1 cup chopped canned tomatoes

1-2 tbsp additional olive oil, for drizzling (optional)

3-4 tbsp cider vinegar, or to taste

2 tsp sugar

½ tsp salt and ½ tsp ground black pepper, or to taste

Pasta with Arrabiata-type Sauce

PREPARATION

For Arrabiata-type Sauce

1 Heat olive oil in a pan.

2 When hot, add asafoetida, chillies or pepper, carrot, salt and black pepper. Sauté for a couple of minutes on a high heat, then add soya mince.

3 Mix in hot water, lower the heat, cover the pan and allow to cook for 5 minutes, stirring occasionally to make sure it does not stick.

4 Turn heat off. Mix in oregano and ground cumin.

For the Pasta

1 Fill a large saucepan with water and bring to a boil.

2 Add the pasta, few drops of oil and salt and allow to cook until almost, but not quite totally, soft – al dente (8-10 minutes, or according to the instructions on the packet).

3 Drain.

(Pasta is best served straightaway to avoid overcooking in its own heat and to prevent sticking together. If this is not possible, reserve some of the drained-off liquid to add to the pasta to warm it up before serving.)

For the Chilli Butter Sauce

In a small saucepan, melt 1 tbsp butter. When hot, add asafoetida, chilli powder and dried mint. Turn off the heat.

To Serve

Place on serving plates and serve the pasta with arrabiata-type sauce, topped with plain yoghurt and a drizzle of chilli butter sauce.

INGREDIENTS

Water for boiling the pasta

2 cups pasta, any kind

Few drops of olive oil

1 tsp salt

1 tbsp butter

1 cup plain yoghurt

Chilli Butter Sauce

Pinch of asafoetida (optional)

1 tsp red chilli powder or flakes

1 tsp dried mint

Arrabiata-type Sauce

2 tbsp olive oil

Pinch of asafoetida

3 green chillies or 1 green bell
 pepper, chopped finely

1 carrot, cut into very small cubes

½ tsp salt and ½ tsp ground black
 pepper, to taste

1 cup soya mince, dry

½-⅓ cup hot water

½ tsp oregano

Pinch of ground cumin

Courgettes and Carrots with Rice Sprinkle

PREPARATION

1 Place the oil in a pan, put on medium to high heat. Add the chopped fennel and sauté for few minutes.

2 Add the carrots and sauté for a further 1 to 2 minutes, then add the courgettes, salt, pepper and rice.

3 After a couple of minutes, add the hot water, reduce the heat to low, cover and allow the vegetables and rice to steam.

4 Check from time to time and stir. If necessary, add a little hot water. Keep covered. Should be cooked in 15 to 20 minutes.

5 When the vegetables are soft, turn off the heat, add finely chopped fresh dill and mint, toss and cover for 5 more minutes.

Alternative: You can add tomatoes (fresh or tinned) at the same time as courgettes, to give a different flavour and colour.

This dish can be eaten hot, warm or cold. You can also serve this with plain yoghurt or with cacik see page 172.

INGREDIENTS

2-3 tbsp olive oil

1 fennel, finely chopped (optional)

3 carrots, peeled, cut quarterly lengthwise and chopped about 2 cm long

4 medium size courgettes, scraped and cut quarterly lengthwise and chopped about 2 cm long

Salt and pepper, to taste

⅓ cup white rice, washed and drained

¼ cup hot water for cooking

1 tbsp fresh dill, chopped very finely

1 tbsp fresh mint, chopped very finely, or 1 tbsp dried mint flakes

Courgettes à la Crème

INGREDIENTS

2 tbsp olive oil

Pinch of asafoetida (optional)

Black pepper, to taste

1 green bell pepper, chopped into 1 cm squares

1 red bell pepper, chopped into 1 cm squares

3 medium to big courgettes, cleaned, halved lengthwise and chopped 1 cm thick

½ tsp granulated sugar

Salt, to taste

3 tbsp plain flour or whole wheat flour

¾ cup double cream

1 cup halloumi cheese, grated coarsely

3-4 tbsp fresh parsley or coriander, chopped

½ cup milk

PREPARATION

1   Preheat the oven to 180°C / 350°F / Gas Mark 4.

2   Heat the oil in a pan. Add asafoetida and black pepper, then add the peppers and sauté for 3 to 4 minutes.

3   Add sliced courgettes, sugar and salt, and sauté for about 5 minutes more. The courgettes should just start to cook and their colour should be fresh green.

4   Turn off the heat, add 3 tbsp of flour and mix together. Put the courgettes in an oven dish.

5   In a bowl, whisk the double cream until smooth, and then add grated halloumi cheese, chopped parsley and milk. Making sure there are no lumps, pour this mixture over the courgettes.

6   Cook in the oven, for about 20 minutes. Turn off the oven when the top gets slightly brown.

You can use any cheese you prefer for this recipe. Halloumi cheese has a salty taste and stays solid even in cooking. It does not melt easily and is therefore excellent for cooking and frying with vegetables.

Falafel-type Burgers

PREPARATION

1 Heat olive oil in a pan on medium to high heat and add the finely chopped chillies or pepper. Sauté for a couple of minutes.

2 Add shredded carrots and sauté for a few more minutes. Reduce the heat to low, add the dry soya mince and mix.

3 Add ½ cup hot water, cover and simmer for 5 minutes. Turn off the heat and allow to cool.

4 In a bowl, mix together the cooked soya mince and the chickpea paste. Add salt, black pepper, oregano, cumin powder, asafoetida, flour and chopped parsley, and form a stiff paste.

5 Shape into narrow flat burgers and shallow fry in the sunflower oil.

6 Put the cooked burgers onto a paper towel to remove excess oil. Serve hot or warm.

Serve with tomato sauce and salad. These burgers can be served together with different kinds of rice and yoghurt as well.

INGREDIENTS

2 tbsp olive oil

3-4 fresh green chillies or 1 green bell pepper, finely chopped

2 carrots, finely shredded

2 cups soya mince, dry

½ cup hot water

1 cup chickpeas, soaked overnight and blended to a smooth paste

½ tsp salt

1 tsp black pepper

1 tsp dried oregano

1 tsp cumin powder

Pinch of asafoetida (optional)

2 tbsp plain flour or oat flour or chickpea flour

3 tbsp fresh parsley, chopped finely

3-4 tbsp sunflower oil, for shallow frying the burgers

Oven Baked Burgers

INGREDIENTS

4 tbsp olive oil

3-4 green chillies or 1 green bell pepper, finely chopped

1 large carrot, very finely grated

1 cup soya mince, dry

½ tsp salt, or to taste

1 tsp black pepper, or to taste

1 tsp cumin

Pinch of asafoetida (optional)

½-¾ cup hot water

½ cup fine wholewheat flour or chickpea (gram) flour

½ cup rolled oats

1 cup rocket, finely chopped, or 1 tbsp ground linseeds mixed with 3 tbsp hot water

½ tbsp tomato paste

PREPARATION

1   Preheat the oven to 180°C / 350°F / Gas Mark 4.

2   Heat the olive oil in a pan. Add chopped green peppers and sauté for couple of minutes.

3   Add carrot and sauté for a further couple of minutes on a high heat.

4   Add dry soya mince and mix well with carrots and peppers until they are bound together.

5   Bring the heat to medium. Add salt, pepper, cumin, asafoetida and hot water.

6   Cover the pan and cook for about 5 minutes, on low heat.

7   Let the mixture cool a little and add flour, oats, chopped rocket or linseed and water mixture, and tomato paste and form a stiff paste. Shape into round patties, about 2 cm thick.

8   Put a small bowl, filled with water, in the heated oven to release steam on the bottom shelf or, if you have steam facility in your oven, set it. (This process will ensure the burgers remain moist and don't dry up.)

9   Bake burgers in the oven for about 15 minutes.

Serve with rice and/or salad or burger buns, see page 160.

Aubergine, Almond and Dill Rice

PREPARATION

1 Heat 2 tbsp butter or oil in a pan. Add almonds and sauté them for few minutes.

2 Add rice and water. Adjust the water to cover the rice and prepare boiling water to add to rice when necessary.

3 The quantity of water needed may vary according to the type of rice. Bring to the boil and then reduce heat to a simmer.

4 Check the rice frequently, adding hot water in very small quantities if required, until the rice is cooked.

5 Remove from heat and use a clean kitchen towel underneath the lid to absorb the steam, which will prevent the rice from becoming soggy.

6 In another pan, fry the aubergine in butter until golden.

7 Add the fried aubergine, finely chopped dill, salt and pepper to the rice and serve.

This recipe comes from Ottoman cuisine and is very frequently cooked in Turkish homes, especially during summer. It goes well with ayran (a drink made by whisking plain yoghurt with water and a little salt) or cacik with dill as on page 172.

INGREDIENTS

2 tbsp butter or olive oil

½ cup almonds, soaked and peeled

1 cup basmati or jasmine rice, washed and drained

About 1½ cup water or enough to cover the rice

1 medium to large aubergine, washed, dried and cut into 2 cm cubes

2 tbsp butter, to fry the aubergines

3 tbsp fresh dill, finely chopped

½ tsp salt and ½ tsp white or ground black pepper, or to taste

Vegetable Biryani

INGREDIENTS

3-4 tbsp olive oil or sunflower oil

1 tsp coarsely ground black pepper or whole black peppercorn

2 pieces cinnamon bark, cut small

6-8 cloves or ½ tsp ground cloves

¾ cup cashew nuts or unsalted peanuts

1 cup white cabbage, chopped very finely

1 carrot, cut into small cubes

¾ cup of cauliflower, cut into very small florets

¾ cup boiled peas

2 cups basmati or jasmine rice

1 fresh tomato, peeled and cut into small cubes

Water

1 tbsp butter (optional)

Fresh coriander, for decoration

PREPARATION

1 Heat the olive oil or sunflower oil in a pan, on a medium to high heat. Add black pepper, cinnamon and cloves. Sauté for a minute and then add nuts.

2 Add finely chopped cabbage and sauté for a further couple of minutes.

3 Add carrot, cauliflower florets and, lastly, peas. Sauté for couple of minutes more.

4 Add washed and drained basmati or jasmine rice, tomato cubes and enough water to cover the surface of the rice.

5 Bring the heat to a simmer and cover. Check the rice from time to time and add hot water in very small quantities, if necessary, until rice is just tender.

6 When the rice is cooked, remove from heat, add a knob of butter to separate the grains and cover.

7 Use a clean kitchen towel underneath the lid to absorb the steam, which will prevent the rice from becoming soggy, and wait for 10 minutes.

8 Before serving, garnish with coriander

This rich rice can be part of a dinner served with plain yoghurt or chutney see pages 180 and 182. You can change the vegetables according to your taste and availability.

147

Many of the vegetarian dishes and soups described in this book are even more delicious when served with a chunk of freshly baked, home-made bread.

Many cultures have their own distinctive breads, traditionally served with particular dishes – in all flavours, shapes and sizes. Made from different grains and flours, there's something for every taste.

SAVOURIES & BREADS

Boreks (Puff Pastry Envelopes)

INGREDIENTS

½ kg puff pastry (ready made frozen)

4 tbsp feta or cottage cheese, grated

4 tsp tomato purée

½ tsp dried basil

¼ tsp black pepper (optional)

Milk for glazing

PREPARATION

1 Defrost the pastry according to the instructions on the packet.

2 Preheat the oven to 180°C / 350°F / Gas Mark 4.

3 For the filling, mix the grated cheese, tomato purée, basil and black pepper.

4 Roll the puff pastry about 2-3 mm thick. Cut 15 cm squares or any other size you want.

5 Fill each pastry square with 1 tbsp of the filling and fold the pastry into triangular, rectangular or envelope-shaped parcels.

6 Triangular and rectangular parcels can be closed by pressing down the edges with a wet fork.

7 Brush milk over top of the boreks.

8 Bake for about 15 minutes in the middle shelf of the oven.

These boreks are very fast to prepare and cook once you have the puff pastry ready to roll. You can be creative with the fillings and prepare: mashed potatoes and peas with a little black pepper and other spices, or grated cheddar cheese with chopped parsley, or stir-fried finely cut vegetables, such as carrot, cabbage, sweetcorn, soya sprouts and soya sauce.

Chilli Biscuits

Makes about 20 – 30 biscuits

PREPARATION

1 Preheat oven to 200°C / 400°F / Gas Mark 5.

2 Grease a baking tray.

3 Sift flour, baking powder, salt, cumin and chilli into a bowl. Rub in butter until the mixture resembles fine breadcrumbs. Make a well in the centre.

4 In a small bowl, whisk the yoghurt and baking powder mixture with the tomato paste and pour into well in the centre of the flour. Mix to form soft dough.

5 Knead dough lightly on a floured surface until smooth.

6 Roll out to ½ cm thick. Using a biscuit wheel or a knife, cut dough into 5 cm squares or any size you prefer.

7 Place on the baking tray. Re-knead and re-roll the trimmings and cut out more biscuits. Continue until the dough is used up.

8 Bake in the oven for 12-15 minutes until very lightly browned.

9 Remove from baking tray to cool on wire racks. Serve with cheese or savoury dips.

Alternative: Roll the dough about 1 cm thick, cut smaller shapes and sprinkle finely grated cheese on top. You can also change the spices or herbs for a variety of tastes.

INGREDIENTS

1½ cups plain flour

½ tsp baking powder

¼ tsp salt, or to taste

1 tsp cumin powder

1 tsp chilli powder, to taste

5-6 tbsp butter, at room temperature

1 tbsp yogurt + 1 tsp baking powder mixed with a fork (to replace 1 egg)

1 tbsp tomato paste

Pitta Bread

Makes 8 – 10 pittas

INGREDIENTS

2 cups self-raising flour

1½ tsp (1 sachet) easy- blend dried yeast

2 tbsp (heaped) natural yogurt

½ tsp salt

1 tbsp oil

4-5 tbsp warm milk or water

A little butter (optional)

A few fresh coriander leaves, for decoration (optional)

PREPARATION

1 Mix the flour, yeast, yoghurt, salt and oil with enough warm milk or water to make a soft dough. Cover and let it rest in a warm place for about 30 minutes.

2 When ready, knead the dough for a few minutes until it is smooth.

3 Then take a small ball of dough, the size of a golf ball, and roll it out to the oval shape of pitta bread. Repeat until you have about 10 pittas.

4 Cook them under a hot grill for 1-2 minutes on each side, until they puff up like balloons. They will flatten as they cool.

5 Brush the pitta with a little butter, garnish with coriander leaves and serve.

Serving suggestions

Pitta bread goes well served with salads and falafel see page 18.

INGREDIENTS

1 cup fine semolina

4 tbsp rice flour

4 tbsp chickpea (gram) flour

4 tbsp natural yoghurt

1 tsp salt, to taste

1 tbsp sunflower or olive oil

1½ cups water

1 carrot, finely shredded

1 cup cabbage, finely shredded

¼ cup red bell pepper, finely
    chopped

¼ cup green pepper, finely
    chopped

¼ cup sweetcorn

¼ cup peas

2 tsp lemon juice

¼ tsp bicarbonate of soda

Green chillies and coriander,
    to taste (optional)

FOR THE TOPPING

Fresh tomato slices, cut round

Cheddar cheese, grated

Green chillies, finely sliced
    (optional)

Fresh coriander, chopped
    (optional)

Savoury Pizza

PREPARATION

1 Place semolina, rice flour and chickpea flour in a mixing bowl. Add the yoghurt, salt, oil and water, and stir the mixture well. The consistency should be like a pancake batter (thick cream). You can add more water if necessary.

2 Mix in the remaining ingredients.

3 Let it stand for about 10 minutes. If you are using coarse semolina, then let the batter stand for 30-40 minutes.

4 Place a flat non-stick frying pan on medium heat (use a pan with a lid or create any other lid which will fit the pan).

5 When hot, pour a couple of ladles of batter into the pan and spread the batter quickly with the back of the ladle.

6 With a spoon, pour a little oil all around the pizza so that it does not stick.

7 Cover the pan and let it cook for a minute or two on a medium to low heat.

8 Turn the pizza over to cook the other side, then place sliced tomatoes and grated Cheddar cheese on top and cover for another minute or so.

9 If you prefer spicy hot pizzas, then add finely sliced green chillies and coriander at the time of adding tomatoes and cheese.

Serve hot - delicious with yoghurt and coconut chutney see page 186.

This is a great party dish which is enjoyed by both children and adults.

Vegetable Pancakes

INGREDIENTS

1 cup bean sprouts

1 cup mushrooms, sliced

2 green chillies or green bell pepper, finely chopped

1 fresh tomato, cubed

2 tbsp fresh parsley or coriander, finely chopped

Pinch of salt, to taste

½ tsp black pepper, or to taste

1-2 tbsp cornmeal

1-2 tbsp plain flour

4-5 tbsp milk or soya milk

Sunflower oil for shallow frying

PREPARATION

1 Put the bean sprouts, chopped vegetables and fresh parsley or coriander into a bowl. Add salt and pepper.

2 Mix in the cornmeal and the plain flour with the vegetables.

3 Pour the milk over the mixture and mix. The flour and milk should be just enough to bind the vegetables together.

4 Heat a non-stick pan on medium to high heat with a little oil.

5 Place a big spoonful of the mixture into the pan and fry both sides.

Serve with cheese and bread and/or salad. You can use any other vegetables available and create varieties. Green chillies can be added for a hotter taste.

Let your good wishes flow like a chocolate fountain.

Makes 10 – 12

INGREDIENTS

1½ tsp instant dry yeast
   (1 sachet)

2 tsp sugar

2 cups warm milk

1 tsp salt

½ cup sunflower oil

1 cup warm water

4-5 cups of plain or
   wholewheat flour (or a
   mixture of both)

Water in an oven-proof bowl
   for cooking

A little milk to glaze

Sesame seeds, for decoration
on top

Burger Buns

PREPARATION

1 Preheat the oven to 50°C / 120°F / Gas Mark less than 0.5.

2 Oil a baking tray.

3 Place the dry yeast in a cup. Add 1 tsp sugar and ½ cup of warm milk. Place the cup in the middle of the bowl in which you'll prepare the dough.

4 Wait for 5 to 10 minutes. The yeast will ferment. (You do need to do this process even though the yeast is instant, because you do not leave the dough for a long time.)

5 Pour the contents of the cup into the bowl, add salt, oil, remaining 1 tsp sugar, remaining 1½ cups of warm milk and 1 cup of warm water, and mix with a spoon.

6 Start adding the flour; it is important that you add the flour little by little, so that you get soft dough which does not stick to your hands. Stop adding flour as soon as you have a nice soft dough.

7 Cover the bowl with a kitchen towel and let the dough rest for 10 minutes.

8 Place the oven-proof bowl, filled with water, at the bottom of the oven. (The steam produced by this small container of water in the oven will keep the bread soft.)

9 At the end of 10 minutes, knead the dough briefly. Take small balls, shape them into perfect rounds and place them on the oiled baking tray, leaving some space in between. Brush the top of the round balls with milk and sprinkle sesame seeds on top.

10 Put the tray in the oven at 50°C. Wait for 10 to 15 minutes for the burger buns to rise.

11 Raise the temperature of the oven to 180°C / 350°F / Gas Mark 4 and cook for 20-30 mins.

These buns are very handy for sandwiches to take away and you may shape them as you like.

Cornmeal Bread

INGREDIENTS

3 cups cornmeal

3 cups wholewheat flour

1 tsp salt

2 tsp baking powder

2 cup milk or soya milk

4 tbsp butter, melted

2 tbsp honey

Olive oil, pinch of thyme and
   pinch of red chilli flakes
   (for serving)

PREPARATION

1   Preset the oven to 180°C / 350°F / Gas Mark 4.

2   Put the dry ingredients into a bowl (cornmeal, flour, salt and baking powder).

3   In a separate bowl, mix together the milk, melted butter and honey.

4   Mix the dry and the liquid ingredients together to form a soft dough.

5   Place the dough in a greased 13 cm x 25 cm loaf tin, or form the dough into a preferred shape. Score the top slightly to assist rising.

6   Place on a baking tray and bake for about 30 minutes.

7   Serve warm, sprinkled with a little olive oil, thyme and chilli flakes.

This bread stays fresh for a few days in an airtight container.

Alternative: For a spicy flavour, add chopped green chillies and coriander at the time of mixing.

Savoury Olive Cake

PREPARATION

1 Preheat the oven to 180°C / 350°F / Gas Mark 4.

2 Mix olive oil, yoghurt and corn flour mixture (to replace 3 eggs) together.

3 Add baking powder, bicarbonate of soda, vinegar, salt and asafoetida, and mix well.

4 Add the black olives, finely chopped peppers, dill, thyme and red chilli flakes.

5 Mix together with the sifted flour.

6 Place the batter in a deep (around 8-10 cm) 20 cm square greased baking tray or a 10 cm x 20 cm loaf tin and bake for 20 to 30 minutes, in the middle shelf of the oven.

Serve with different cheese slices along with tea, for an extended Sunday breakfast or as a light lunch accompanying a salad.

Also handy to take on picnics or for packed lunches.

INGREDIENTS

½ cup olive oil

½ cup plain yoghurt

Mixture of 3 tbsp corn flour + 3 tbsp yoghurt + 3 tbsp water or milk (to replace 3 eggs)

1 tsp baking powder

1 tsp bicarbonate of soda

1 tsp cider vinegar or any other vinegar

½ tsp salt

Pinch of asafoetida (optional)

20 black olives, pitted and sliced

2-3 green chilli peppers or 1 green bell pepper, finely chopped

3 tbsp dill, freshly chopped

1 tsp thyme

1 tsp red chilli flakes (optional)

2 cups plain flour or wholewheat flour, sifted

Poachas (Turkish Cheese Savouries)

PREPARATION

1 Preheat the oven to 180°C / 350°F / Gas Mark 4.

2 Mix olive oil, yoghurt, baking powder, bicarbonate of soda, vinegar and salt.

3 If you are using chopped fresh dill, then, add it at this stage to the dough.

4 Another alternative is to decorate the poachas with sesame seeds at a later stage.

5 Start by adding one cup of flour and mix. Continue to add and mix in each cup of flour slowly, until a soft dough is formed. (The flour quantity needed may vary according to the kind of flour.)

6 Form patties of about 10 cm diameter by patting golf-ball sized dough flat. Or form big patties, according to your preference.

7 Add the filling to the middle and fold over to form 'D' shapes.

8 Close the ends by pressing with your fingers. Brush with milk. (Place sesame seeds on top for decoration at this stage).

9 Place the poachas on a slightly oiled baking tray, leaving 2-3 cm distance in between.

10 Bake for about 25 minutes in the middle shelf of the oven.

Goes well with tea or can be eaten for breakfast or with soups.

INGREDIENTS

1 cup olive oil

1 cup plain yoghurt

1 tsp baking powder

1 tsp bicarbonate of soda

1 tsp cider vinegar (or any other vinegar)

½ tsp salt

5 cups plain flour or wholewheat flour or mixture of both

Milk for glazing

2 tbsp finely chopped dill or 2 tbsp sesame seeds, for decoration

FOR THE FILLING

3-4 medium sized mashed potatoes, 3-4 tbsp chopped parsley and black pepper mixed, or

1 cup grated feta or cottage cheese, and 3-4 tbsp finely chopped parsley mixed, or

Any other filling you prefer, making sure that it is not too moist

A good meal can be turned into a great meal when accompanied by a perfectly complementing chutney.

The vegetarian shopping basket offers a fabulous range of flavours to be combined with subtlety and skill into exquisite chutney – sweet or sour, sharp or spicy. This chapter also includes delicious dips that are great party fare with crudités, sticks of fresh cut salad vegetables.

CHUTNEYS & DIPS

Mayonnaise

INGREDIENTS

½ cup olive oil

½ cup milk or soya milk

Juice of 1 lemon

Pinch of salt

Mustard and/or asafoetida, to taste (optional)

PREPARATION

1 Blend together the olive oil and milk, using a hand blender.

2 Add lemon juice in very small amounts to the mixture and continue mixing with the blender. Stop adding lemon juice when the required consistency is achieved.

3 Continue adding more lemon juice if the required consistency is not achieved. Take care that the mayonnaise does not turn runny. If it becomes runny, add a little oil.

4 Add salt and mustard and/or asafoetida to taste and serve.

Keeps well in the fridge for a few days.

Cacik with Dill

PREPARATION

1 Peel and de-seed the cucumber. Chop into very small cubes or grate coarsely.

2 Add all the ingredients to the yoghurt and mix well with a fork.

3 Put into bowls, decorate with fresh dill and serve cold.

Especially in hot summer days, cacik is very refreshing as a side dish, accompanying rice dishes or vegetables.

INGREDIENTS

½ cucumber

2 tbsp fresh dill, chopped finely

2 tbsp fresh mint, chopped finely

2 cups plain yoghurt

Pinch of asafoetida (optional)

1 tbsp olive oil

Salt and pepper, to taste

Dill for decoration, optional

Respect oneself and every living creature
– that is the recipe for a good life.

Home-made Yoghurt

INGREDIENTS

2 cups milk (either semi-skimmed or full cream)

1 tbsp natural yoghurt

Lassi is made from equal quantities of home-made yoghurt and water, mixed with a whisk or electric mixer. You can either add salt for salty or sugar for sweet lassi.

Also freshly ground cumin seeds can be added to the salty lassi. In India, especially in summer months, this refreshing drink is served with meals and aids digestion.

PREPARATION

1 Boil the milk in a stainless steel pan. Let it cool a little.

2 It is important to have the correct temperature, and so it's better if you use a thermometer and ensure the temperature is 105°F to 110°F (40°C to 43°C).

3 Add the yoghurt. Mix well and cover with a lid.
(If not using a stainless steel pan, transfer the yoghurt to a bowl and cover).

4 Leave to set in a warm place overnight. The ambient temperature should be 90°F to 100°F (33°C to 38°C). A good place is next to the boiler or hot water storage cylinder, otherwise incubate in a warm oven for about 8 to 12 hours.

5 In hot weather, it will set in 8 hours so there's no need to put it in a warm place.

6 When set, place in the fridge.

7 Home-made yoghurt is best consumed fresh daily, as it turns sour very quickly.

Fava-Broad Bean Purée

PREPARATION

1 If you use fresh broad beans, shell them and boil the beans. If using dried broad beans, add enough water to cover.

2 Check from time to time and if needed add extra hot water in small quantities (to prevent boiling dry) until the beans are completely soft.

3 Combine all the ingredients together with a blender. Place the purée in a bowl and serve with additional olive oil on top.

4 Broad bean purée can be served with cut vegetables as a dip or as a spread with breads.

INGREDIENTS

1 cup dry broad beans or 2 cups fresh broad beans

Water for boiling

4 tbsp olive oil

1 tbsp Greek yoghurt (optional, for a lighter texture)

½ tsp salt, or to taste

½ lemon, freshly squeezed, or to taste

A pinch of asafoetida (optional)

1 tsp granulated sugar

1-2 tbsp chopped fresh dill (optional)

1 tbsp additional olive oil, for decoration

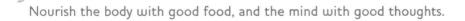

Nourish the body with good food, and the mind with good thoughts.

Spicy Tomato Spread

INGREDIENTS

1 cup tomato paste

½ cup olive oil

½ cup walnuts, coarsely chopped

½ tsp salt, or to taste

1 tsp dried mint

½ tsp cumin powder

½ tsp dried thyme

½ tsp chilli powder

Pinch of asafoetida (optional)

PREPARATION

1   Mix all the ingredients together. Use as a spread.

2   You can keep this spread in a jar in the fridge for about 1 week.

Alternative: Instead of chilli powder, you can use fresh red chillies according to your taste.

Be sparing with spices, let good fresh food speak for itself.

Coriander Chutney

PREPARATION

1 Put all the ingredients in a food processor, together with 2 tbsp water (or more if you prefer a thinner green chutney). Blend to a smooth paste.

2 Serve in a decorative shallow dish.

Note: You can prepare this chutney a few days in advance and it stays fresh in the fridge for a few days. It can stay in the freezer for a few weeks.

INGREDIENTS

2 cups fresh coriander, washed and chopped

3-4 green chillies

Fresh ginger, peeled and cut into pieces 2.5 cm long

1 tsp of sugar and 1 tsp of salt, to taste

½ tsp cumin powder

1-2 tsp lemon juice

2 tbsp water

Spicy Tomato and Red Pepper Chutney

INGREDIENTS

2 big fresh tomatoes

2 tsp tomato paste (optional)

½ red bell pepper

I or 2 red or green chilli peppers

2.5 cm piece of cucumber

2.5 cm piece of carrot

1 tsp salt, or to taste

1 tbsp vinegar or lemon juice

1 tsp cumin powder

PREPARATION

1   Put all the ingredients in a food processor, and blend to a smooth paste.

2   Serve in a decorative shallow dish.

Note: This versatile chutney stays fresh in the fridge for a few days.

It is ideal with burgers and falafel see pages 106, 108, 140 and 142.

Yoghurt and Mint Dip

PREPARATION

Mix all the ingredients together in a bowl and serve.

Note: This is a very easy and quick dip to make, it goes well with all the potato dishes and is also tasty with cut vegetable sticks (celery, carrots, cucumber).

INGREDIENTS

4-6 tbsp natural yoghurt

2 tsp bottled mint sauce or 2 tsp finely chopped fresh mint

½ tsp salt, to taste

Yoghurt and Coconut Chutney

INGREDIENTS

4-6 tbsp natural yoghurt

1 tbsp desiccated coconut

2 green chillies, finely chopped

½ tsp salt and tsp sugar, to taste

1 tbsp sunflower oil

1 level tsp mustard seeds

1 tbsp fresh coriander leaves, washed and chopped finely

¼ tsp asafoetida

3-4 curry leaves

1-2 tsp dhal, mung or urad (optional)

PREPARATION

1 Mix yoghurt, dessicated coconut, green chillies, salt and sugar together in a bowl.

2 Place a small pan on the stove, put in the oil and, after a few seconds, add the mustard seeds and cover with a lid.

3 After the mustard seeds have popped, put in the coriander leaves, asafoetida, curry leaves and dhal (if using) for a few seconds. Then turn off the heat.

4 Mix this oil mixture into the yoghurt mixture and stir well.

Note: This is versatile chutney and is delicious with savoury pizza see page 156. It also goes well with the wraps on page 24.

The serene mind that prepares food creates serenity within those who then eat.

While we're all conscious of the health implications of too much sugar or fat, there is nothing like a mouth watering dessert to round off a good meal. And there are sweets and puddings here to enjoy as a regular healthy addition to a nutritious meal, along with some for very occasional treats. Ideas, too, for sweets that can be presented as gifts for special occasions.

SWEETS & TREATS

Cream Cheese Cake

INGREDIENTS

FOR THE CAKE:

1 cup flour

½ cup melted butter

1 tbsp honey

½ cup sugar

½ cup milk

FOR THE CREAM:

2 cups (500 gms) mascarpone cheese

8 tbsp icing sugar

Vanilla essence or powder, to taste

6 tsp fresh lemon juice

Pomegranate seeds and lemon zest, for decoration

PREPARATION

1 Preheat the oven to 180°C / 350°F / Gas Mark 4.

2 Mix all the cake ingredients together to form a dough.

3 Roll to the shape of the baking tray, either square or rectangular, or 2 cm round in diameter. Prick some holes in the dough with a fork, to ensure better cooking.

4 Bake for about 12 to 15 minutes, until light brown. Take care that the cake is not cooked any longer as it gets hard.

FOR THE CREAM:

1 Mix the mascarpone cheese, icing sugar, vanilla essence or powder, and lemon juice to a cream with a hand whisk.

2 Place the layer of the cake base onto a serving plate. Spread the cream on top, using a large knife or spatula.

3 Decorate with pomegranate seeds and lemon zest (or with other soft fruits, according to taste).

If you prefer a more crumbly base, than follow the recipe for Hearty Cookies on page 204.

Very tasty and easy cake to impress your guests at parties.

Wholemeal Tahini Cake

PREPARATION

1 Preheat the oven to 170°C / 335°F / Gas Mark 3.5.

2 Mix together the cornflour, yoghurt and milk mixture (to replace eggs) and honey until smooth.

3 Add the butter and whisk with a blender for 3 minutes.

4 Mix in the tahini.

5 Add milk, walnuts, sugar, flour, baking powder, bicarbonate of soda, cinnamon and, finally, vanilla and salt.

6 Grease a 25 cm round cake tin, or use a greaseproof lined loaf tin, and pour in the cake mixture.

7 Bake in the middle shelf of the oven for about 40 minutes (insert a skewer in the middle of the cake and if it comes out clean the cake is ready).

8 Leave to cool before turning out of tin.

9 Sprinkle icing sugar on top (optional) and serve.

INGREDIENTS

Mixture of 3 tbsp cornflour + 3 tbsp yoghurt + 3 tbsp milk (to replace 3 eggs)

1 cup honey

5 tbsp butter, at room temperature

1 cup tahini

1 cup milk

½ cup walnuts, coarsely chopped

4 tbsp brown sugar

2 cups wholewheat flour, sifted

1 tsp baking powder

1 tsp bicarbonate of soda

1 tsp ground cinnamon

1 tsp vanilla powder or 2 tsp vanilla essence

½ tsp salt

Icing sugar for decoration (optional)

Golden Nut Biscuits

INGREDIENTS

3 cups plain flour

1½ cups sugar

250gms butter or margarine, at room temperature

Mixture of 3 tbsp yoghurt + 3 tbsp milk + 3 tbsp cornflour (to replace 3 eggs)

2 tbsp yoghurt

1 tsp bicarbonate of soda

1 tbsp cider vinegar

Hazelnuts or walnuts, for decoration

PREPARATION

1 Preheat the oven to 180°C / 350°F / Gas Mark 4.

2 Mix flour, sugar and butter or margarine in a large bowl, to the consistency of fine breadcrumbs.

3 Blend the yoghurt, milk and cornflour mixture with a fork or whisk in a separate bowl and add to the flour mixture.

4 Add 2 tbsp of yoghurt, bicarbonate of soda and cider vinegar, mixing well with hands to form a soft dough.

5 Take small walnut-sized pieces from the dough and roll into perfect rounds. Arrange in a greased baking tray, allowing about 10 cm distance between them as they will flatten and spread whilst baking.

6 Place a hazelnut or half a walnut on top of each biscuit.

7 Bake on the middle shelf for about 20 minutes. Check the biscuits do not brown.

8 The biscuits will be soft when taken out of the oven and will harden as they cool.

9 When cooled a little, place biscuits on a cooling wire rack and cover with a clean tea towel until totally cool and ready to serve or store.

Semolina Pudding

PREPARATION

1 Place the butter, milk, semolina and sugar in a pan on a medium heat. Cook, stirring continuously, until the mixture boils.

2 Turn the heat to low, add the essence or rose water and allow to boil for no longer than 1 to 2 minutes.

3 The mixture may seem runny at this point, but it will set as it cools.

4 Grease a glass dish, 30 x 30 cm square, with a little melted butter, or wet the dish, and pour the mixture in and allow it to cool, first at room temperature and then in the fridge.

5 For topping, mix the walnuts, brown sugar, desiccated coconut and cinnamon. Sprinkle on top to decorate.

6 Cut into squares or diamond shapes.

Alternative: Prepare a double measure of all the ingredients and pour half of the semolina pudding first, then sprinkle half of the topping material, then pour the rest of the semolina pudding and decorate the top. If you choose to do this, you will have a more fancy dessert which you can serve for your guests.

Feel free to use any tray you wish to adjust the depth of your semolina pudding.

INGREDIENTS

1 tbsp butter

3½ cups milk

8 tbsp semolina

8 tbsp sugar

Few drops of vanilla or almond essence, or rose water

DECORATION:

½ cup walnuts, chopped

¼ cup brown sugar

¼ cup desiccated coconut

1 tbsp ground cinnamon

Dark Brown Chocolate Cake

INGREDIENTS

1¾ cup plain flour

¾ cup cocoa powder

2 cups sugar

1½ tsp baking powder

1½ tsp bicarbonate of soda

½ tsp salt

Large pinch of vanilla powder
or 1 tsp vanilla essence

1 cup milk

½ cup sunflower oil

1 cup water, hot

White chocolate flakes

PREPARATION

1 Preheat the oven to 180°C / 350°F / Gas Mark 4.

2 Sift the flour into a mixing bowl. Add all the dry ingredients (cocoa powder, sugar, baking powder, bicarbonate of soda, salt and vanilla) and mix.

3 Mix all the liquid ingredients (milk, sunflower oil and hot water) in a separate bowl.

4 Mix the dry and the liquid ingredients together and whisk briefly with a hand whisk.

5 Bake in an oiled 30 cm diameter cake tin or 30 cm x 30 cm square tray at 180°C for about 40 minutes, or until a skewer or knife inserted into the cake comes out clean.

6 Leave to cool. (This is a very soft wet cake and you might need to cut the cake into squares and serve from the tin/tray.)

7 Decorate with white chocolate flakes.

This is delicious served warm or cold, with vanilla ice cream or cream and decorate with fresh mint.

Fat-free Fresh Fruit Muffins

Makes around 12 muffins

PREPARATION

1 Preheat the oven to 180°C / 350°F / Gas Mark 4.

2 Mix all the dry ingredients together (flours, sugar, baking powder, bicarbonate of soda, cinnamon, linseed and salt).

3 Mix the milk with the lemon juice and pour it into the dry ingredients. Stir until just moistened and take care not to over stir.

4 Add in the fresh fruit pieces.

5 Spoon the mixture into muffin tray moulds that have been oiled to prevent sticking. If you need to use paper cases, then you need to oil them or the muffins will stick to the cases.

6 If you use topping, mix the topping ingredients together. Top each muffin with an equal amount of the mixture.

7 Bake for about 15 to 20 minutes, until a toothpick or skewer inserted comes out clean.

8 Allow to cool before removing from the cases, then serve.

This is a very practical and healthy muffin recipe as it is fat-free.

INGREDIENTS

1 cup plain flour

1 cup wholewheat flour

½ cup sugar

1 tsp baking powder

¾ tsp bicarbonate of soda

½ tsp ground cinnamon

1 tbsp ground linseed

Small pinch of salt

1 cup milk

2 tbsp lemon juice

1 cup peeled or unpeeled fresh fruit, such as berries, peaches, or any other soft fruits, cut into small cubes

OPTIONAL TOPPING

1 tbsp plain flour

¼ cup brown granulated sugar

3 tbsp nuts, coarsely grated

½ tbsp sunflower oil

½ tbsp water

Healthy Sweet Fruit Cream

INGREDIENTS

1 cup plain yoghurt

1-1½ tbsp honey

½ tsp cardamom powder, to taste

1 tsp vanilla powder or 2 tsp vanilla essence

1 cup or more diced fresh fruits, such as peach, banana, pear, mango, melons etc. according to taste and season.

Individual or mixed fruits can be used.

PREPARATION

1   Mix all the ingredients, except the fruit, with a hand whisk.

2   Once the other ingredients are blended, add the fruit, mix lightly and serve.

This is a very quick, light and appetising sweet at any time of the day, especially on hot summer days.

When the cook is sweet, so is the food.

Hearty Cookies

Makes about 15 to 20 cookies

PREPARATION

1   Pre-heat the oven to 180°C / 350°F / Gas mark 4.

2   Mix first the sugar and the butter together and then add all the other ingredients, (except the flour) and mix.

3   Add the flour slowly, starting with 2 cups and adding in more as you need. Keep on adding flour until a soft dough is formed.

4   Roll the dough out to about 1.5 cm thick and cut with a heart-shaped cutter. Continue rolling and cutting until all the dough finishes. (Or you can adjust the thickness according to your preference.)

5   Place the cookies on a baking sheet and cook for about 30 minutes or until golden. Ensure that they do not turn brown.

6   Remove from oven, cool on wire cooler. You can decorate with icing sugar as an option.

For variety you can add cinnamon and cardamom to the dough, and the cookies can be made into any shapes and sizes/thin or chunky according to your liking.

They keep well in an airtight container for a couple of weeks.

INGREDIENTS

10 tbsp sugar

250gms butter, at room temperature

½ cup sunflower oil

½ cup plain yoghurt

1 tbsp orange juice and 1 tbsp grated orange zest

1 tsp soda bicarbonate

½ cup coarsely ground walnuts or pistachios

1 tsp vanilla powder or 2 tsp vanilla essence

4-5 cups plain flour

Icing sugar for decoration (optional)

Semolina Halva with Almonds

INGREDIENTS

2 cups water

1 ½ cups sugar

1 tsp ground cinnamon

⅓ cup whole almonds with or without skin

⅓ cups pistachio nuts

3 tbsp butter

1 cup semolina

PREPARATION

1   Heat the water, sugar and cinnamon in a saucepan until the sugar is completely dissolved. Keep this syrup aside.

2   As an option, you may refrain from including the cinnamon in the syrup but sprinkle on top of the halva when ready.

3   Toast the almonds and pistachios in a dry pan.

4   Melt the butter in a separate pan and sauté the semolina on medium heat in the butter. Keep stirring, until brown.

5   Add the toasted almonds and pistachios.

6   Add in the syrup. Keep stirring until the water is absorbed which will take roughly 8 to 10 minutes.

7   Decorate and serve warm.

Semolina halva is a sweet dish made for every occasion, such as celebrations, as well as for family meetings and even funerals, throughout East and Middle East Countries. Also, in India, this delicious dessert is offered at religious festivals.

Fruit Crêpes

PREPARATION

FOR THE CRÊPES:

1 Mix the milk and the flour and whisk by hand to a smooth texture.

2 Place the pan on medium heat and melt ¼ tbsp butter. Add a large spoonful of crêpe mixture to the pan, distribute the batter evenly to the pan to get the crêpe as thin as possible and fry each side.

FOR THE FILLING:

1 Cook on medium heat, for about 10 to 15 minutes the fruit cubes with sugar, vanilla and cardamom (optional).

2 Do not cover. Stir from time to time. The fruits should first give out their juices and then resemble a consistency close to jam.

3 Spoon the fruit filling onto the crêpe and roll. Sprinkle icing sugar on top, before serving.

Best when served warm and still crispy.

FOR THE CRÊPES

1 cup milk

5 tbsp plain flour

Butter for cooking

Icing sugar for decoration

FOR FILLING

2 cups fresh fruit cubes or slices, such as peach, banana, berries, raisins, strawberries etc.

4 tbsp sugar

½ tsp vanilla powder or 2 tsp vanilla essence

½ tsp ground cardamom (optional)

Icing sugar for decoration

Super Carrot Cake

INGREDIENTS

2 cups plain flour

1 cup sugar

2 medium carrots, finely grated

½ cup sultanas or raisins

1 cup walnuts, coarsely chopped

¼ tsp vanilla powder or 1 tsp vanilla essence

1 tsp ground cinnamon

1 tsp baking powder

½ cup sunflower oil

1 cup milk

PREPARATION

1 Preheat the oven to 180°C / 350°F / Gas mark 4.

2 Mix the dry ingredients - flour, sugar, carrots, sultanas, walnuts, vanilla, cinnamon and baking powder.

3 Mix together the oil and milk in a separate bowl.

4 Fold the liquid into the dry ingredients, using a large stirring spoon.

5 Grease or cover with a baking paper a deep 25 cm x 30 cm baking tray and pour the mixture into the tray.

6 Bake for about 40 minutes.

This cake is rich in aroma and becomes a moist carrot cake, and lasts up to 2 weeks in an airtight containers.

💬 Success on the table is a measure of orderliness in the kitchen.

Banana Chocolate Chip Cake

PREPARATION

1 Preheat the oven to 180°C / 350°F / Gas mark 4.

2 Mix mashed bananas with mixture of yoghurt, water and corn flour (replaces 2 eggs).

3 Add sifted flour, sugar, bicarbonate of soda, ground cinnamon, vanilla and sunflower oil, and mix well with a fork or hand whisk. Mix in ¾ of the chocolate chips to the batter.

4 Pour batter into a greased cake tin. Sprinkle with demerara sugar or cinnamon mix, and the remaining chocolate chips.

5 Bake for 30 to 40 minutes or until a skewer inserted into the cake comes out clean.

Alternative: You can omit the sunflower oil and use the same method to make banana chocolate bread.

INGREDIENTS

3 ripe bananas, mashed

2 tbsp plain yoghurt, 2 tbsp water and 2 tbsp corn flour, mixed together (replaces 2 eggs)

1 cups plain flour, sifted

1 cups sugar

1 tsp bicarbonate of soda

1 tbsp ground cinnamon

1 tsp vanilla powder or vanilla essence

⅓ cup sunflower oil

1 cup chocolate chips

¼ cup demerara sugar or coarse sugar mixed with a little cinnamon, for decoration on top (optional)

Simplicity in the kitchen creates clarity in the mind.

INGREDIENTS

FOR THE FRUIT FILLING

2 tbsp butter

2 apples, washed, peeled and sliced

2 pears, washed, peeled and sliced

½ cup sultanas, rinsed and dried

4-5 whole cloves

1 tbsp ground cinnamon

1 banana, peeled and chopped

1 cup blueberries

½ cup chopped nuts (walnuts, hazelnuts or almonds)

FOR CRUMBLE

4 tbsp butter, at room temperature

2 cups of plain flour

1 cup of brown sugar

Mixed Fruit Crumble

PREPARATION

1   Preheat the oven to 180°C / 350°F / Gas Mark 4.

2   To prepare the fruit filling, place 2 tbsp of butter in a pan. Add the apples, pears, sultanas, whole cloves and ground cinnamon.

3   Sauté for a few minutes on a high heat. Turn the heat to medium and cook for 5 minutes.

4   Add the banana, blueberries and chopped nuts to the mixture. Place mixture in an oven dish.

5   To prepare the crumble, combine the butter, flour and sugar in a bowl. The mixture should have the consistency of fine breadcrumbs. (You can add more flour if the consistency is moist and not crumbly.)

6   Spread the crumble on the layer of fruit and bake in the oven for about 30 minutes, until the crumble turns golden.

7   Serve with vanilla, or any other, ice cream or double cream.

You can use just apples or any fruit in season. A very practical, delicious and quick dessert.

Panna Cotta

PREPARATION

1   Mix all the ingredients in a pan and cook, stirring continuously, on medium heat until the mixture boils.

2   Pour into wet moulds and leave to cool, and then place in the fridge for a few hours to set.

3   Mix the ingredients for the topping and pour on the panna cottas, before serving.

Alternative: You can use rose essence or saffron as alternative to vanilla essence, whilst preparing panna cotta, for a variety of flavours.

INGREDIENTS

1 cup milk

¾ cup double cream

4 tbsp sugar

½ cup water

1 tsp agar agar powder

FOR TOPPING (Optional)

1 tbsp honey

3 tbsp water

⅔ tsp vanilla essence

Puff Pastry Parcels with Apricot Jam

INGREDIENTS

Flour, to use for rolling the puff pastries

½ kg puff pastry

1 cup apricot jam (or any other jam available)

A little milk for brushing

PREPARATION

1 Preheat the oven to 200°C / 400°F / Gas Mark 5.

2 Sprinkle flour onto the working surface where you will roll the puff pastry. Cut the rested and softened puff pastries into 4 pieces. Roll them out, to 2 – 3 mm thick.

3 Cut the rolled pastry into squares and/or rounds.

4 Place the jam in the middle of squares or rounds. Fold the squares as envelopes and rounds as 'D' shapes. Press the 'D' shapes with a wet fork to seal the ends.

5 Cut thin pastry strips from the leftover rolled pastries and place on top of the 'D's as if you were tying a parcel. Brush the top of the parcels with milk.

6 Place the parcels on the oven tray. You don't need to oil the tray.

7 Place the tray in the middle shelf and cook for about 15 to 20 minutes until golden brown.

8 When cooled, you can sprinkle icing sugar on top, if you want to decorate the parcels further.

These parcels are elegant treats for teatime with friends or relaxed Sunday brunches.

Sugarless Dried Fruits and Nuts Treat

Makes around 20 to 25

PREPARATION

1 Wash the dried fruits with warm water, making sure there are no stones in any of the fruits. Grind them in the food processor or chop them into small pieces.

2 Roast the nuts in a pan over the stove, stirring all the time, until the cashew nuts become light golden brown; or roast in the oven. When cool, grind them coarsely. Put them aside.

3 Melt the butter in a pan on a low heat. Then add the chopped fruits and keep stirring until the fruits become soft.

4 Add the nuts and mix well. Turn off the heat, add cardamom, mix and make into shapes using moulds or by hand.

5 Store in the fridge.

These are a healthy treat and they last in the fridge for 2 to 3 weeks.

Use only dates with nut for a sweeter taste.

These sweets make a lovely gift to share with friends and family.

INGREDIENTS

2 cups dried fruits (pitted dates, figs and apricots)

1 cup mixed nuts (cashew nuts, almonds and pistachios)

2 tbsp unsalted butter

1 tsp cardamom

Sweet Energy Balls

INGREDIENTS

1½ cups rolled oats

4 tbsp sesame seeds

⅓ cup honey

⅓ cup tahini

½ cup walnuts or any other nuts, chopped into small pieces

Chopped pistachios, for decoration

PREPARATION

1　Mix all the ingredients together.

2　Let the mixture rest in the fridge for ½ to 1 hour.

3　Form the mixture into balls and decorate with pistachios and serve.

Stays fresh for a week when stored in the fridge.

Alternative: Roast the rolled oats and sesame seeds together, add in the other ingredients and, without needing to set the mixture in the fridge, form rolls. Decorate with pistachios and serve.

The unroasted preparation method is healthier for the seeds and nuts in general, but the roasted method might be tastier.

These sweets can be presented in gift boxes to friends...

Vermicelli Pudding

PREPARATION

1 Place the butter and vermicelli in a pan, and fry for few minutes on a high heat. Be careful that the vermicelli does not burn, as it can do so quickly.

2 Turn the heat to medium. Mix in the raisins or sultanas, sugar or honey, and milk.

3 Add the rice flour, ground cardamom and vanilla, stirring continuously.

4 Boil, then reduce heat to very low and simmer for 2 minutes.

5 Put into serving bowls and decorate with nuts. Serve warm or cold.

INGREDIENTS

1 tbsp butter

4 tbsp vermicelli, crushed

2 tbsp raisins or sultanas

4 tbsp sugar or 3 tbsp honey

4 cups milk

4 tbsp rice flour

1 tsp ground cardamom

1 tsp vanilla powder or 2 tsp vanilla essence

Chopped nuts for decoration

Plain food from those who love us tastes better than the fancy food of strangers.

Walnut Cake

INGREDIENTS

4 cups plain flour

½ tsp vanilla powder or essence

1 tsp ground cinnamon

1½ tsp baking powder

¾ cup honey

2¼ cups warm black tea

¾ cup sunflower oil

1 cup sugar

1 cup walnuts, coarsely chopped

PREPARATION

1 Preheat the oven to 170°C / 335°F / Gas mark 3.5.

2 Sift the flour into a bowl. Add vanilla powder, cinnamon and baking powder, and mix. (If you use vanilla essence, mix it with liquid ingredients instead.)

3 In a separate bowl, mix honey and warm tea, until the honey dissolves. Add sunflower oil and sugar, and mix again briefly.

4 Mix the dry and the liquid ingredients together and whisk briefly by hand. Mix in the walnuts.

5 Cook in an oiled 30 cm diameter baking tin of or 30 cm x 30 cm square deep tray for about 50 minutes, or until a toothpick or skewer inserted into the cake comes out clean.

6 Leave to cool for about 10 minutes before turning out of tin.

7 Serve with cream.

This cake is very light and easy to make. It is also suitable for a vegan diet.

Quick Fruit Fix

PREPARATION

1. Cut the apples, pear, plums and peaches into small pieces; no need to peel them.

2. Place the cut fruits into a pan on medium heat, add caster sugar and allow them to cook. Do not cover.

3. Add the berries approximately 5 minutes later. Add cloves and/or cardamom, if you want to use them, at this point.

4. Once the fruit mix starts boiling, turn off the heat. Do not overcook.

5. Prepare the cream by whisking the yoghurt, the double cream, vanilla essence and icing sugar together.

6. Serve when the fruits are warm or cold.

This is a quick and easy treat, which can help when you feel a craving for sweets and a fruit does not seem enough to satisfy your need.

You can experiment using other fruits, except acid fruits such as oranges, lemons etc.

INGREDIENTS

1-2 apples

1 pear

2-3 plums

2-3 peaches

½ cup caster sugar

A handful of mixed berries

Cloves and/or ground cardamom, optional

FOR THE CREAM

1 cup Greek yoghurt

3-4 tbsp double cream

2 tsp vanilla essence

2-3 tbsp icing sugar

Makes around 15 to 20 cookies

INGREDIENTS

5 tbsp icing sugar

250gms butter, at room temperature

¼ cup sunflower oil

3-4 cups plain flour

½ tsp ground cinnamon

1 tsp vanilla powder or 2 tsp vanilla essence

Icing sugar, for decoration

Crumble Cinnamon Cookies

PREPARATION

1 Preheat the oven to 170°C / 335°F / Gas mark 3.5.

2 Cream the sugar, butter and sunflower oil together, using a fork or hand whisk.

3 Add 2 cups of flour to start with, ground cinnamon and vanilla, and mix to form dough. Add the remaining flour little by little and stop as soon as you can form small balls by hand, taking care not to knead too much.

4 Arrange the balls on a greased baking tray, leaving some room between the balls for them to rise.

5 Bake in the middle shelf for about 20 minutes. Watch to ensure that they do not brown too quickly.

6 When cool, decorate with icing sugar.

This is a very traditional Turkish cookie to serve your guests for tea.

As an alternative shape, you can roll ropes of 3 to 4 cm diameter and cut 4 cm length and press flat with a fork to get square cookies with a striped top decoration.

Chocolate Vegan Cake
(with Courgettes)

PREPARATION

1 Preheat the oven to 170°C / 335°F / Gas Mark 3.5.

2 Sift the flour into a mixing bowl. Add cocoa powder, vanilla and baking powder, and mix together.

3 Add sugar and sunflower oil, and mix lightly.

4 Add bicarbonate of soda and lemon juice, and mix briefly.

5 Add grated courgettes and mix, then add soda water and whisk briefly by hand.

6 Finally, add walnuts.

7 Cook on an oiled 15 cm x 30 cm rectangular deep tray or greaseproof lined loaf tin at 170°C for about 50 minutes, or until a skewer inserted into the cake comes out clean.

8 Allow to cool before removing from the tray.

The courgettes give a special texture to the cake and nobody can guess this special ingredient until they are told. This is a light and tasty dark chocolate cake to be enjoyed at any time.

INGREDIENTS

2 cups plain flour

½ cup cocoa powder

½ tsp vanilla powder or essence

1½ tsp baking powder

1 cup sugar

½ cup sunflower oil

1 tsp bicarbonate of soda

Few drops of lemon juice

2 medium size green courgettes, grated coarsely and liquid squeezed out (it is important that the courgettes are as dry as possible)

½ cup fizzy soda water

½ cup walnuts, chopped coarsely

Makes 8

INGREDIENTS

16 sheets of filo pastry

8 tbsp brown sugar

8 tbsp walnuts or hazelnuts, coarsely ground

4 ripe bananas, medium to firm consistency, peeled and cut in half lengthwise

1-2 cups sunflower oil, for deep frying

2-3 tbsp honey

Banana Parcels

PREPARATION

1 Place 2 sheets of the filo pastry together on a work surface. Sprinkle all over with 1 tbsp of brown sugar and 1 tbsp of ground nuts.

2 Place a banana half on each pastry piece, fold in from two sides first and roll along the long side to make a parcel.

3 Dampen the pastry ends slightly and press together to seal.

4 As an alternative, you can roll the banana parcels as triangle packs; in this case, mash the bananas coarsely.

5 Heat sunflower oil in a deep pan on medium to high heat and fry the pastry pieces on both sides until golden brown.

6 You can also bake the banana parcels, but the banana filling gets a little too soft in this case.

7 Remove and blot with paper towels to remove excess oil. Leave to cool slightly.

8 Drizzle with honey and serve.

This is a quick and satisfying sweet after a light meal.

INGREDIENTS

1 kg fresh apricots

1¾ cups caster sugar

Few whole cloves (optional)

Pinch of vanilla powder (optional)

Few drops of lemon juice or ½ tsp citric acid

Apricot Jam

PREPARATION

1 Pit and cut the apricots into small pieces. Place them in a pan.

2 Add the caster sugar on top and start cooking on medium heat. Do not cover. The fruit will produce its own juice.

3 Mix with a wooden spoon from time to time but do not overdo it. Once the mixture starts boiling, bring the heat to low, add the cloves, vanilla and few drops of lemon juice or citric acid.

4 Allow the jam to cook slowly. The colour of the apricots will become darker orange and the consistency will be thick.

5 Then you can turn the heat off. Place the jam in a sterilised jar filled to the top and keep in the fridge to consume in 1 or 2 weeks.

If you want the jam to last for a long time, you can make the jars airtight by following the directions below.

1 You need to put the jam into sterilised jars while the jam is still boiling. Fill the jars to the top, wipe the surface of the jar opening then close the lid immediately.

2 Turn the jars upside down and let them cool overnight.

3 The next day, see if there is any leakage. If there is leakage, you need to repeat the process of boiling the jam once again and placing it into jars and keeping the jars upside down one more time overnight. If there is no leakage, keep the jam jars on a cool dark place. Once you open the jam jar, keep it in the fridge and consume in 2 to 3 weeks.

The same recipe can be used for plums and peaches. You can use the apricot jam to fill the puff pastry parcels on page 218 as a nice tea-time treat.

Simple Baklavas

Makes 15-20 pieces

INGREDIENTS

¾ cup coarsely ground mixed nuts
   (almonds, pistachios, cashew nuts)

½ cup Demerara Sugar

1 tsp ground cardamom

5-6 tbsp melted butter

6 sheets filo pastry

VARIATION

You can also make them into rolls, which are easier, by sprinkling the nut and sugar mixture on to the brushed uncut pastry. Carefully make a roll and cut them into desired size pieces.

If you prefer a sweeter taste or you want to have special baklavas, then, after removing them from the oven, you can pour some honey over each baklava and decorate with ground pistachios. Or you can dust the baklavas with icing sugar when cooled.

PREPARATION

1 Preheat the oven to 150°C / 300°F / Gas Mark 2.

2 Mix the nuts, sugar and cardamom in a bowl.

3 Melt the butter in a small pan.

4 Take 6 sheets of filo pastry and brush each sheet with melted butter.

5 Lay down all the sheets on top of each other on a flat working surface (e.g. chopping board). With a sharp knife, cut into squares of 4 cm.

6 Onto each square of pastry, put about 1 heaped teaspoon of the nut and sugar mixture, then fold up four corners to the centre and make the pastry into the shape of a flower.

7 Arrange them on a small baking tray, making sure they are close to each other so the pastry ends do not open up too much.

8 Bake in the middle of the oven for about 25min or until golden brown.

They make lovely gifts to give on special occasions

Soft Lemon Cookies

Makes 15 to 20 cookies

PREPARATION

1. Preheat the oven to 180°C / 350°F / Gas Mark 4.

2. Mix all the ingredients together, except the icing sugar, by the following method to form soft dough.

3. Be careful with the flour and start by mixing 2 cups first and gradually add more as you form the dough. Stop adding in the flour as soon as you have soft dough.

4. It is always important to mix the flour little by little, as the quantity required might change according to the type of flour used.

5. Roll the dough 1½ cm thick and cut out the cookies with a biscuit cutter. Place the cookies on an oven tray, apart from each other as they will expand.

6. Bake in the middle of the oven for about 15 minutes or until golden. Do not overcook them.

7. After the cookies are baked and cooled, sprinkle icing sugar on top to decorate (optional).

8. This cookie is slightly less sweet. If you prefer a sweeter taste, you can increase the amount of sugar.

A lovely treat at teatime and they stay fresh in an airtight container for a couple of weeks.

INGREDIENTS

2½-3 cups plain flour

1 cup corn flour

4 tbsp sugar

250gms butter or margarine, at room temperature

1 tbsp plain yoghurt

1 tsp baking powder

1 tsp vanilla powder or 2 tsp vanilla essence

Finely grated zest of 1 lemon

Icing sugar, for decoration (optional)

Orange Dessert with Honey and Vanilla Cream Sauce

INGREDIENTS

2 medium sized fresh oranges

1 tbsp honey

3 tbsp orange juice, freshly squeezed

2 tbsp Greek yoghurt

2 tbsp icing sugar

1 tbsp double cream

1 tsp vanilla powder or 2 tsp vanilla essence

Pistachios to decorate

PREPARATION

1 Peel the oranges, removing skin and pith. Cut into round slices of about 1 cm thick.

2 Place the slices on a serving plate. Mix the honey and orange juice and pour onto the orange slices.

3 Mix the yoghurt, icing sugar and cream together using a hand whisk, add vanilla and use to decorate the orange slices.

4 Sprinkle with pistachios and serve.

This is a very refreshing and easy to make treat.

Gratitude is a great accompaniment to any meal: just say, "Thank You."

Carrot Rolls with Coconut

Makes 14 to 16 rolls

PREPARATION

1 Put the butter in a pan on a medium heat. Add the grated carrots, cinnamon, vanilla and cardamom, and sauté for few minutes.

2 Add sugar and sauté for 1 more minute.

3 Add the cornflour and mix together. Cook for few minutes.

4 Turn off the heat and add the nuts. Let the mixture sit until it cools.

5 Moisten hands and form rolls. Cover them with desiccated coconut and serve.

Store in the fridge.

INGREDIENTS

2 tbsp butter

3 medium to large carrots, finely grated

Pinch of cinnamon

½ tsp of vanilla essence

Pinch of ground cardamom

8 tbsp sugar

2 tbsp cornflour (or any other starch)

4 tbsp walnuts or any other nuts, coarsely ground

Desiccated coconut, to cover the rolls

Agar Agar

Globe Artichoke

Asafoetida

Aubergine

Coriander

Red Chilli Flakes

Green Chilli Peppers

Dill

Linseed

Coriander Seeds

Mint

Okra/Ladies Fingers

Parsley

Cardamom

White Kidney Beans

Cinnamon

Cloves

Walnuts

Yoghurt

Chickpeas

Ingredients

AGAR AGAR

is a gelatinous substance obtained from the cell walls of some species of red algae or seaweed. It can be used as a vegetarian gelatine, a thickener for soups, in jellies, ice cream and Japanese desserts .

This natural additive is prepared from several species of red algae. It has high gelling properties, and is used by vegetarians because true gelatine is made from calves' feet.

Agar agar forms a gel at 88°F and does not melt below 136°F. It is unflavoured and is rich in iodine and trace minerals. Agar agar's setting properties are stronger than unflavoured gelatine and will set at room temperature after an hour. It is a high protein food and should therefore be refrigerated for storage.

ARTICHOKE

The globe artichoke is related to the thistle. Its leaves are edible, as is the bottom part of the flower, called the heart (which you can also buy tinned or frozen). Globe artichokes make a delicious starter simply boiled whole and served with melted butter, mayonnaise or vinaigrette for dipping the leaves.

Break off each leaf and draw the soft fleshy base through your teeth. Once you've removed all the leaves, you can pull or slice off the hairy 'choke' and then eat the heart and the bottom with the remaining sauce.

The recipe given in the book is prepared with the artichoke heart.

How to clean and prepare artichokes for cooking
You will need cold water, two washed lemons and artichokes.

Have a large bowl at hand, containing cold water and the juice of two lemons together with the four discarded lemon halves with rind (lemon water). Keep the artichokes in another bowl of cold water while you are working on them.

Take one artichoke at a time, drain it, and pull off and discard the smallest outer leaves. Holding the artichoke with its bottom towards the little finger of your hand, tilt the top away from you and, holding a small sharp knife tightly with your right hand, insert the knife tip, one leaf deep, into the tender, lighter part of the leaves. Keeping your right hand steady, slowly rotate the artichoke with your left hand, so the bottom moves in a clockwise direction, and cut upward in a spiral. The tough part of each leaf will fall off, while the tender edible part remains attached. Peel the green layer off the bottom and stem, and then drop the trimmed artichoke into the lemon water until you are ready to cook.

This operation requires some practice; you will know if you have mastered this technique when the artichoke thus cleaned looks more or less like the one you started with, only smaller and whiter.

If you are not ready to use the artichokes immediately after you have cleaned them, try to keep them completely submerged in lemon water. This is not easy as artichokes are very buoyant and float to the surface making it difficult to keep them covered. An inverted plate, just a bit smaller in diameter than the bowl, placed over the artichokes, will keep them below the surface. Another way is to crowd them inside a glass jar and cover them with the lemon water. If you plan to leave them at this stage for more than an hour or so, you must refrigerate them, but it is not advisable to keep artichokes this way for more than a few hours. Lemon is used to prevent discoloration; but the lemon will cause the artichokes to spoil very quickly.

ASAFOETIDA (HING)

Asafoetida is a plant from the Apiaceae family, which includes carrots, parsley, dill, celery, caraway, fennel and lovage. Native to the Middle East, asafoetida is a perennial plant that grows about six feet (1.83 m) high and bears bright yellow clusters of flowers. The hollow stem and roots of the asafoetida plant house a milky resin substance that is rich in organic sulphur. This resin is dried and blended with rice flour to create a flour that is used in cooking. Today, the most commonly available form is compounded asafoetida, a fine powder containing 30% asafoetida resin, along with rice flour and gum arabic.

Though it smells offensive, asafoetida tastes much like a combination of strong onions with a touch of earthy truffles. Its odour is so strong that it must be stored in airtight containers otherwise the aroma, which is nauseating in quantities, will contaminate other spices stored nearby. However, its smell becomes much milder in cooking.

The rich, distinctive taste is popular with daring cooks who will find asafoetida an interesting alternative to onion and garlic, even for Western dishes. Careful small dosage is, though, essential. In ancient Rome, asafoetida was stored in jars together with pine nuts, where the nuts alone were used to flavour delicate dishes. Another method is dissolving asafoetida in hot oil and adding the oil drop by drop to soups and stews. If used with sufficient moderation, asafoetida enhances mushroom and vegetable dishes, including stir-fry.

According to the Ayurveda, a more than 2,000 year old comprehensive system of medicine based on an holistic approach rooted in Vedic culture, asafoetida is considered to be a highly useful digestive, disinfectant, antispasmodic, mild diuretic, a stimulant for glandular secretion, an aid to circulation and is particularly useful for strengthening the nerves.

Asafoetida has been used as a medicinal herb for many decades, with some people choosing to make a tea from it in order to drink it. Despite its pungent aroma, asafoetida is known to alleviate stomach ailments, cold symptoms, anxiety issues, chronic fatigue, yeast infections and painful gas and flatulence.

AUBERGINE

Although the plump, pear-shaped variety, with its near-black shiny-skinned exterior, is probably most familiar in Britain, aubergine come in a wide variety of shapes, colours and sizes. Aubergines can be bought all year round but they are at their best, not to mention cheapest, from July to September. Look for unblemished, firm, lustrous skin with a bright green calyx, or stem.

One of the reasons why some people overlook aubergine is the bitterness that is characteristic of old varieties. The newer breeds no longer demand salting and draining (which draws out any bitter juices), although this process has one advantage: an initial salting takes away the tendency of aubergine to soak up oil when then cooked, resulting in a less greasy meal. And frying, roasting or grilling is what you must do to savour its creamy flesh; throwing it raw into a dish is a waste of aubergine.

CHILLI: RED CHILLI FLAKES

Dried capsicum flakes used to season food.

Red chilli flakes are also known as: crushed red pepper, dried chilli flakes, chilli flakes, red pepper flakes .

CHILLI: GREEN CHILLI PEPPERS

Chilli peppers are popular in food. They are rich in vitamin C and are believed to have many beneficial effects on health.

DRIED BEANS and PEAS

The easiest way to cook dried pulses like chick peas and kidney beans is to soak them beforehand for about 8 to 10 hours or overnight. Before cooking, remove any bean or pea that appears discoloured.

Extra care must be taken to cook kidney beans so they are completely soft before eating. Otherwise they may still contain toxin that can cause a bad stomach upset.

Add a half teaspoonful of bicarbonate of soda to the water when cooking all dried beans and peas, as this accelerates the cooking time.

OKRA / LADIES FINGERS

Okra is now widely available but some times people are put off cooking them as the vegetable releases slime.

Here are some suggestions for handling okra in order to avoid this happening.

While okra is still whole, rinse thoroughly, pat completely dry with a clean towel or disposable paper towel. (Always wash and dry okra after cutting as the water contact will release the slime.)

Place whole pods (fingers) in freezer bags to freeze solid overnight. Cook from frozen making sure it does not thaw even a little, as water contact encourages the slime to come out.

Alternatively, cook okra in a pan with a tablespoonful of white vinegar or lemon juice. This process 'burns' the slime leaving the okras slime-free to season according to your taste.

In the same way, the slime on your hands can be removed by rinsing them with a dash of vinegar or lemon juice.

Cook okra in a heavy pot in a couple of tablespoons of oil. Once cooked you can flavour them.

WALNUTS

Walnuts are rich in oil and are widely eaten both fresh and in cookery. Walnut oil is expensive and consequently is used sparingly; most often in salad dressing.

Walnuts are also an excellent source of omega-3 fatty acids and have been shown as helpful in lowering cholesterol. They need to be kept dry and refrigerated to store well; in warm conditions they become rancid in a few weeks, particularly after shelling.

LINSEED

Also called flaxseed, this seed is a variety of the common flax, Linum usitatissimum, grown for its yield of linseed oil and meal.

High in Omega-3, essential fatty acids, linseed is the richest source of lignin. Flaxseed oil is known to help reduce cholesterol, support skin and intestinal integrity and help maintain a healthy digestive, immune and nervous system.

OLIVE OIL

Olive oil is a fruit oil obtained from the olive (Olea europaea), a traditional tree crop of the Mediterranean Basin. It is commonly used in cooking, cosmetics, pharmaceuticals, soaps and as a fuel for traditional oil lamps. Olive oil is considered a healthy oil because of its high content of monounsaturated fat (mainly oleic acid) and polyphenols.

Due to its chemical structure, olive oil is best suited for human consumption. Its excellent digestibility promotes the overall absorption of nutrients, especially vitamins and mineral salts. It has a positive effect on constipation.

Promoting bone mineralisation, it is excellent for infants and the elderly who have bone calcification problems. It also has beneficial effects on brain and nervous system development as well as overall growth. It shields the body against infection and helps in the healing of tissues internal or external.

YOGHURT

Yoghurt is a dairy product produced by bacterial fermentation of milk. Fermentation of the milk sugar (lactose) produces lactic acid, which acts on milk protein to give yoghurt its texture and its characteristic tang. Yoghurt substitutes can be made from soya milk.

Yoghurt has nutritional benefits beyond those of milk: people who are lactose-intolerant often enjoy yoghurt without ill effects, apparently because live yoghurt cultures contain enzymes which help break down lactose inside the intestine.

Yoghurt also has medical uses, in particular for a variety of gastrointestinal conditions and in preventing antibiotic-associated diarrhoea.

Yoghurt is customarily made in domestic environments in regions where yoghurt has an important place in traditional cuisine. It can be made from a small amount of store-bought, plain, live culture yoghurt by adding milk and heating at a constant, but not boiling, temperature. Special yoghurt-making machines assist in small-batch yoghurt-making.

HERBS

PARSLEY

Parsley is a very healthy and tasty fresh herb used abundantly in Mediterranean cooking. Since it has a stronger flavour than the curly variety, Italian flat leaf parsley holds up better to cooking and therefore is usually the type preferred for dishes served hot. It should be added towards the end of the cooking process so that it can best retain its taste, colour and nutritional value.

Choose fresh parsley that is deep green in colour and looks fresh and crisp. Avoid bunches that have leaves that are wilted or yellow as this indicates that they are either over mature or damaged.

Fresh parsley should be washed just before using since it is highly fragile. The best way to clean is to place it in a bowl of cold water and swish it around with your hands. This will allow any sand or dirt to dislodge. Remove the leaves from the water, empty the bowl, refill it with clean water and repeat this process until no dirt remains in the water. Dry, if possible before cutting.

CORIANDER

Coriander is a delicate annual herb with several branches and lacy leaves with jagged edges, belonging to the carrot family. Coriander's leaves, called cilantro, are used as seasoning in curries, salads and soup and its dried ripe spherical seeds, mostly in powder form, are slightly roasted and used as curry powder in dishes, to flavour cakes and cookies. This fragrant spice also has its own medicinal properties.

How to store: store in refrigerator with cut ends in a jar of water and leaves loosely covered with a plastic bag for several days. Change water every 2 days. Or cut the ends and store in a plastic bag wrapped in kitchen paper for a week.

Matches well with: avocado, breads, ice cream, lentils, mayonnaise, peppers, rice, salads, tomatoes, yogurt.

MINT

Mint leaves have a pleasant warm, fresh, aromatic, sweet flavour with a cool aftertaste. Mint leaves are used in cuisine to add aroma to the dishes and mostly used along with parsley and/or dill. Mint also aids digestion.

DILL

Dill, a member of the parsley family, is a strong-smelling, fennel-like plant. The flavour is destroyed in heating so it is added at the end of cooking. It goes especially well with vegetables like courgettes, potatoes, carrots, peas, sauces, yoghurt and cream. Dill adds refinement to the taste of vegetable dishes prepared with olive oil and served warm.

SPICES

SEEDS or POWDERS?

Whenever possible, buy whole seeds (e.g. cumin, coriander) instead of powder, since powder loses its flavour more quickly and the seeds can be easily ground with a mortar and pestle.

Even though dried herbs and spices are widely available in supermarkets, explore the local spice stores or ethnic markets in your area. Often these stores feature an expansive selection that is of superior quality and freshness compared to those offered in other shops. Just like with other dried spices, try to select organically grown since this will give you more assurance that it has not been irradiated.

Both seeds and powder should be kept in a tightly sealed glass container in a cool, dark and dry place. For instance, ground cumin will keep for about six months, while the whole seeds will stay fresh for about one year.

CLOVES

Cloves are the aromatic dried flower buds of a tree. It is native to Indonesia and used as a spice in cuisine all over the world.

CARDAMOM

Cardamom has a strong, unique taste, with an intensely aromatic fragrance. It is a common ingredient in Indian cooking, and is often used in baking in Nordic countries. One of the most expensive spices by weight, little is needed to impart the flavour. Cardamom is best stored in pod form, because once the seeds are exposed or ground, they quickly lose their flavour. However, high-quality ground cardamom is often more readily (and cheaply) available, and is an acceptable substitute. For recipes requiring whole cardamom pods, a generally accepted equivalent is 10 pods equals 1½ teaspoons of ground cardamom.

CINNAMON

Cinnamon is the inner bark of a tropical evergreen tree.

Cinnamon comes in 'quills', strips of bark rolled one inside another. The pale brown strips are generally thin, the spongy outer bark having been scraped off. The best varieties are pale and parchment-like in appearance. Cinnamon is very similar to cassia, and in North America little distinction is given, though cassia tends to dominate the market.

Cassia and cinnamon have similar uses, but since it is more delicate, cinnamon is used more in dessert dishes. It is commonly used in cakes and in other baking milk and rice puddings, chocolate dishes and fruit desserts, particularly apples and pears.

GRINDING THE SPICES

Whole spices can be ground in a small coffee grinder, small food processor, pepper grinder or mortar and pestle.

To clean the coffee grinder after use, add a small amount of sugar and process. Then discard the sugar.

Simple Measurement Chart

Cooking Measurement Abbreviations

Abbreviation	Measurement
Tsp	teaspoon
Tbsp	tablespoon

1 cup	Liquid 237 ml
	Flour, icing sugar 100 grams
	Caster sugar, rice, lentils 200 grams
	Semolina 165 grams
	Wheat, chick peas, kidney beans 180 grams
	Cornflour, riceflour 120 grams
	Broad beans 150 grams
1 tablespoon	Butter 15-20 grams
	Rice 15 grams
	Flour 7.5 grams
	Semolina 12 grams
	Granulated sugar 15 grams
	Icing sugar 8 grams
	Salt 18 grams
	Cornflour, riceflour 6.5 grams

Temperature Conversion

Fahrenheit to Celsius:
Subtract 32, Multiply by 5, Divide by 9

Celsius to Fahrenheit:
Multiply by 9, Divide by 5, Add 32

Cooking Measurements

Granny's Measurements

Measurement	Equivalent
a Dash	1/4 teaspoon
a Pinch	1/8 teaspoon
1/4 stick butter	2 tablespoons
1 stick butter	1/2 cup
juice of a lemon	3 tablespoons
juice of an orange	1/2 cup

Cooking Measurement Equivalents

Measurement	tsp	tbsp	fl oz	cup	pint	quart	gallon
tsp	1	1/3	1/6	1/48			
Tbsp	3	1	1/2	1/16	1/32		
oz	6	2	1	1/8	1/16		
cup	48	16	8	1	1/2	1/4	1/16
pint	96	32	16	2	1	1/2	1/8
quart	192	64	32	4	2	1	1/4
gallon	768	256	128	16	8	4	1

DRY or WEIGHT Measurements (approximate)

1 ounce		30 grams (28.35 g)
2 ounces		55 grams
3 ounces		85 grams
4 ounces	1/4 pound	125 grams
8 ounces	1/2 pound	240 grams
12 ounces	3/4 pound	375 grams
16 ounces	1 pound	454 grams
32 ounces	2 pounds	907 grams
1 kilogram	2.2 pounds / 35.2 ounces	1000 gram

Liquid or Volume Measures (approximate)

1 teaspoon		1/3 tablespoon	5 ml	
1 tablespoon	1/2 fluid ounce	3 teaspoons	15 ml	15 cc
2 tablespoons	1 fluid ounce	1/8 cup, 6 teaspoons	30 ml	30 cc
1/4 cup	2 fluid ounces	4 tablespoons	59 ml	
1/3 cup	2 2/3 fluid ounces	5 tablespoons & 1 teaspoon	79 ml	
1/2 cup	4 fluid ounces	8 tablespoons	118 ml	
2/3 cup	5 1/3 fluid ounces	10 tablespoons & 2 teaspoons	158 ml	
3/4 cup	6 fluid ounces	12 tablespoons	177 ml	
7/8 cup	7 fluid ounces	14 tablespoons	207 ml	
1 cup	8 fluid ounces/ 1/2 pint	16 tablespoons	237 ml	
2 cups	16 fluid ounces/ 1 pint	32 tablespoons	473 ml	
4 cups	32 fluid ounces	1 quart	946 ml	
1 pint	16 fluid ounces/ 1 pint	32 tablespoons	473 ml	
2 pints	32 fluid ounces	1 quart	946 ml	0.946 litres
8 pints	1 gallon/ 128 fluid ounces	4 quarts	3785 ml	3.78 litres
4 quarts	1 gallon/128 fluid ounces	1 gallon	3785 ml	3.78 litres
1 litre	1.057 quarts		1000 ml	
128 fluid ounces	1 gallon	4 quarts	3785 ml	3.78 litres

Cooking Methods

SAUTÉ

Sautéing is a method of cooking food that uses a small amount of fat in a shallow pan over relatively high heat. Food that is sautéed is usually cooked for a relatively short period of time over high heat, with the aim of browning the food while preserving its colour, moisture and flavour. One may sear simply to add flavour and improve appearance before another process is used to finish cooking it.

When sautéing, it is important that (1) the oil is preheated so that the food browns well and doesn't absorb the oil; 2) the pan is low sided and large enough to hold the food without crowding so that the food browns quickly rather than stewing in its own juices; and (3) the food to be cooked is completely dry to prevent it from stewing.

During sauteing, the golden rule is to stay with the food. If you must walk away, just remove the pan from the stove and finish it later.

DEEP FRY

Deep-frying is a cooking method whereby food is submerged in hot oil or fat. This is normally performed with a deep fryer, chip pan or wok.

Deep frying is classified as a dry cooking method because no water is used and, due to the high temperature involved and the high heat conduction of oil, it cooks food extremely fast. If performed properly, deep-frying does not make food excessively greasy because the moisture in the food repels the oil: the hot oil heats the water within the food, steaming it from the inside out.

As long as the oil is hot enough and the food is not immersed in the oil for too long, oil penetration will be confined to the outer surface. However, if the food is cooked in the oil for too long, too much of the water will be lost and the oil will begin to penetrate the food. The correct frying temperature depends on the thickness and type of food, but in most cases it lies between 175°C and 190°C (345°F – 375°F).

One practical way to test the frying temperature is to place a small piece of bread in the oil, and observe that it turns golden brown in 10-15 seconds.

While frying, don't crowd foods in the pan or the temperature will drop and the food will absorb more oil.

SHALLOW FRY/PAN FRY

Shallow frying is the cooking of food in a small amount of fat or oil in a shallow pre-heated pan, or on a metal surface, at a high temperature. Shallow frying is a skilful process that requires constant care and attention. The result should be crispy and lightly browned with little evidence of fat.

The purpose of shallow frying is 1) to improve the taste of prime foods; 2) to add different texture to food through browning; and 3) to cook food quickly, usually for immediate consumption.

As a form of frying, shallow / pan frying relies on oil as the heat transfer medium and the correct temperature to retain the moisture in the food. The exposed topside allows, unlike deep frying, some moisture loss and contact with the pan bottom creates greater browning. Because of the partial coverage, the food must be flipped over at least once to cook both sides.

The advantages of using less oil are practical: less oil is needed on hand and time spent heating the oil is also much shorter.

Generally, a shallower cooking vessel is used for this method. Using a deep pan with a small amount of oil does reduce spatter but the increased moisture around the cooking food is generally detrimental to the preparation.

TOAST or DRY ROAST

This process can accentuate the taste and aroma of spices such as cumin, coriander, and nuts and seeds such as pine nuts, almonds, sunflower seeds, sesame seeds.

To toast, heat a heavy shallow pan over medium heat until hot. Add spice(s); toast 2 to 5 minutes or until spices are fragrant and lightly browned, stirring or shaking the pan constantly to prevent burning. Remove from heat.

You may wish to bear in mind that although toasting/roasting greatly enhances the taste, it does reduce the nutritional value of the seeds and nuts.

BRAHMA KUMARIS WORLD SPIRITUAL UNIVERSITY

The Brahma Kumaris World Spiritual University is an international organisation working at all levels of society for positive change. Established in 1937, the University now has more than 8,500 centres in over 100 countries.

Acknowledging the intrinsic goodness of everyone, the University teaches a practical method of meditation that helps people better understand their inner strengths and values and put them into practice in their own lives. Courses and seminars encourage spirituality in daily living and include positive thinking, overcoming anger, stress-free living and self-esteem. These are also brought into healthcare, social work, education, prisons and other community settings.

The University's Academy for a Better World in Mount Abu, Rajasthan, India, offers individuals from all walks of life opportunities for life-long innovative learning. The University also supports the Global Hospital and Research Centre in Mount Abu.

Local centres around the world provide courses and lectures in meditation and positive values, helping individuals to recognise their inherent qualities and abilities, and make the most of their lives.

All courses and activities are offered free of charge.
www.bkwsu.org

WORLD HEADQUARTERS
PO Box No 2, Mount Abu 307501, RAJASTHAN, INDIA
Tel: (+91) 2974 - 238261 to 68, Fax: (+91) 2974 - 238952
E-mail: abu@bkivv.org

**INTERNATIONAL CO-ORDINATING OFFICE &
REGIONAL OFFICE FOR EUROPE AND THE MIDDLE EAST**
Global Co-operation House, 65-69 Pound Lane,
London, NW10 2HH, UK
Tel: (+44) 208 727 3350, Fax: (+44) 208 727 3351
E-mail: london@bkwsu.org

AFRICA
Global Museum for a Better World, Maua Close,
off Parklands Road, Westlands, Po Box 123, Sarit Centre,
Nairobi, Kenya
Tel: (+254) 20-374 3572, Fax: (+254) 20-374 3885
E-mail: nairobi@bkwsu.org

AUSTRALIA AND SOUTH EAST ASIA
78 Alt Street, Ashfield, Sydney, NSW 2131, Australia
Tel: (+61) 2 9716 7066, Fax: (+61) 2 9716 7795
E-mail: ashfield@au.bkwsu.org

THE AMERICAS AND THE CARIBBEAN
Global Harmony House, 46 S. Middle Neck Road
Great Neck, NY 11021, USA
Tel: (+1) 516 773 0971, Fax: (+1) 516 773 0976
E-mail: newyork@bkwsu.org

RUSSIA, CIS and THE BALTIC COUNTRIES
2 Gospitalnaya Ploschad, build. 1, Moscow - 111020, Russia
Tel: (+7) 495 263 02 47 Fax: (+7) 495 261 32 24
E-mail: moscow@bkwsu.org